ST

DOCUMENTS OF MOD

General Editor:

A. G. Dickens

Germany in the Thirty Years War

Gerhard Benecke

EDWARD ARNOLD

© Gerhard Benecke 1978

First published in Great Britain 1978 by
Edward Arnold (Publishers) Ltd,
41 Bedford Square, London WC1B 3DQ

Edward Arnold (Australia) Pty Ltd,
80 Waverley Road, Caulfield East,
Victoria 3145, Australia

Reprinted 1984 (with additions to bibliography), 1986

ISBN 0 7131 6135 3

Printed and bound in Great Britain by
The Camelot Press Ltd, Southampton

Contents

Preface

My interest in the subject was first aroused by Mr A. F. Upton at St Andrews through the writings of Francis Carsten.

I should like to thank several groups of special-subject students for their critical approach to the problems of a 'crisis of the German Empire, 1600–50'. They were provided with earlier versions of this collection of documents. The members of a research seminar into early modern German History at Kent in 1974–5, as well as Herbert Würster of the University of Regensburg, must also be thanked. The documents printed here are only a minute portion of the rich materials still to be uncovered at source in central European archives and libraries. For all their help I am grateful to the archivists and librarians of the Staatsarchiv and Landesbibliothek at Detmold in Lippe-Westphalia, the Haus-, Hof- und Staatsarchiv in Vienna, Kungliga Biblioteket, Stockholm, the British Library and the Institute of Historical Research, London, the Cambridge University Library, and the Libraries and Inter-Library Loan Departments of the University of Kent at Canterbury and the University of British Columbia in Vancouver. For sub-editing I am grateful to my wife, Karin, and for typing to the secretaries in Darwin College, above all to Mrs Sue Macdonald. The collection remains my own responsibility. The work is dedicated to Brigitta.

Gerhard Benecke

Canterbury, October 1977

Note on translation

Where an obviously valuable English version exists, this has been used, but most translations are new, often taken from more readily accessible up-to-date German versions or reprints, to which reference is made at the end of each document. Sometimes Baroque German can be untranslatable unless it is paraphrased, and the point of translation has been to emphasize readability and vividness wherever possible. Readers of German are asked to bear this in mind when referring back to original texts.

Illustration

The illustration on the jacket/cover is by Hanns Ulrich Franck (1603–75), master painter of the haberdashers' guild in Augsburg from 1637. It opens a series of twenty-five etchings on *The Fortunes of War*, executed between 1643 and 1656 probably in emulation of the work of Jacques Callot. The title page, reproduced here, was done last and captioned:

O höre nimb in acht
     dz gegenwertig
betracht dz künfftig Vnnd vergess halt nit
Dass fertig

Listen and take a warning from the present
Contemplate the future
And never forget the past.

The central character is a mercenary in all his finery, balancing on a ball of fortune and flanked by civilians pleading poverty, seizing false opportunity and ending in destitution.

Chronology

the other side. Exclusion of Spain, whose war with France continues until 1659. Papal refusal to accept the religious peace.

1653–4   Last Imperial assembly to be held in the *ad hoc* manner maintained since the constitutional reforms of the fifteenth century. All instances of federal government in law, taxation and defence re-established in some form or another. Effective end of 'The Thirty Years War' for the territories of the Holy Roman Empire of the German Nation.

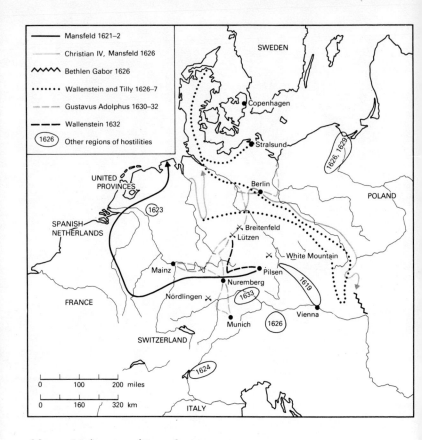

Map 1: Main campaigns, 1619–32

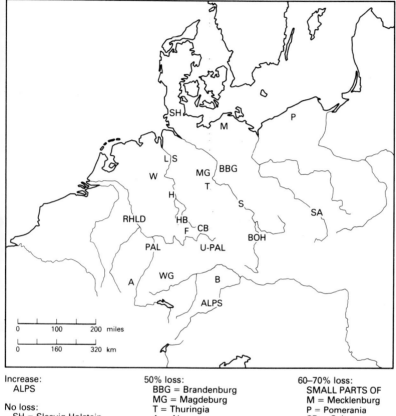

Increase:
  ALPS

No loss:
  SH = Slesvig-Holstein
  LS = Lower Saxony
  W = Westphalia
  RHLD = Rhineland

20% loss:
  SA = Silesia
  BOH = Bohemia

50% loss:
  BBG = Brandenburg
  MG = Magdeburg
  T = Thuringia
  A = Alsace
  B = Bavaria
  F = Franconia
  S = Saxony
  U-PAL = Upper Palatinate

60–70% loss:
  SMALL PARTS OF
  M = Mecklenburg
  P = Pomerania
  CB = Coburg
  HB = Henneberg
  H = Hesse
  PAL = Palatinate
  WG = Württemburg

Map 2: Population loss

Figures and terminology (i.e. 'loss') are crude and vague and must be used with caution. Overall rural loss through war, migration and disease *may* have been up to 40 per cent and in the towns possibly one third.

Coinage and measures

Coinage

1 pound = $\frac{1}{2}$ gulden

1 gulden (fl) = 4 ort

               15 batzen

               40 schilling

               60 kreuzer (kr)

1 (reichs) taler (rtlr, tlr) = $1\frac{1}{2}$ gulden

                              $22\frac{1}{2}$ batzen

                              90 kreuzer

This excludes debased coins circulating between 1620 and 1624. In 1622, for example, 1 rtlr = 6–15 gulden.

Dry measures

1 sester = 875 grams

1 imen = 84 kilos

1 malter = approx. 120 kilos

1 metzen = 5 litres (dry measure)

Liquid measures

1 mass (measure) = approx. $1\frac{1}{3}$ litres

1 eimer (bucket) = 120 mass

                        approx. 165 litres

1 fuder = 12 eimer

          approx. 2,000 litres

Introduction

> The German war, the Thirty Years War, was a part of a general European problem which has yet to be studied properly as a phenomenon in *European* history.
> Henry Kamen in *European History, 1500–1700*.

> The war from outside is dangerous to us, yet the war within even more so.
> Translated from a letter by the Lippe Estates' politician, Henrich Grote, to Levin von Donop, 18 November 1635.

The problems of war and peace which the German Empire and the component territories experienced in the first half of the seventeenth century cannot be understood monocausally. Nor can they be comprehended any more easily by pluralistic explanations, if by pluralism one merely recounts one thing after another and tells the story. We must seek to understand the interplay of religious and secular factors, together with the complexities of local and territorial, national and supranational, dynastic and elective, civil and military developments. To impose a rationale on the period is essential for the clarity and sense of the argument, and this may be attempted by accentuating some basic types of interpretation. The first is religious and patriotic. The second is economic.

A religious interpretation is the most common explanation available from the chronicles, news-sheets, year-books and official propaganda of the period. War and pestilence were interpreted from the pulpit as the wrath of God, righteously and inscrutably meted out to poor sinners who made up the Euro-Christian system of belief at the time, whether Tridentine Catholic, Lutheran, Calvinist or Sectarian. The chronicles, often compiled by the clergy at parish and local institutional levels, as well as their sermons (where they have survived), bring out this fatalism to be remedied in work, prayer and betterment of conscience and action. To deny the strength of this religious mentality as a basis for the thoughts and actions of those who lived in the period is to exaggerate the power of secular and dynastic politics, with its gamut of ambitious diplomats, ministers, soldiers and officials at territorial or supraterritorial courts, chancelleries, treasuries and government centres. Of course, the one fed the other and they were inextricably entwined. We must remember that religion was all-embracing, and if politicians like Richelieu or military enterprisers like Wallenstein could handle it cynically, then they still needed it all the more as an effective ideology in order to induce support for their decisions among subjects and ordinary people. Politics without religion was unthinkable. Naturally, religion had its own development: it was an all-pervading ideology of the times and always changing with circumstances despite the continuity of much of its terminology and first principles. To that extent we might return to saying that the Thirty Years War was a religious conflict if only because that is how the majority of people living through the period regarded the matter. The secular-diplomatic and military dimensions of war were themselves an essential part of this religious overview, and necessarily so, for it gave antagonists and protagonists ammunition for the war in people's minds, manifesting divine retribution by imposing a *Kriegsraison* (reason of war) on the German-speaking people within their loose federation of territories as an essential prelude to a more effective *Staatsraison* (reason of state) and territorial state sovereignty.

Added to this religious dimension was the prejudice of patriotism, a love of territory and locality which could sometimes develop into xenophobia, especially when natives played unwilling host to Croat, Spanish, Swedish, Italian, French regiments and the like. By taking into account the feelings of the period in this way, we can make value judgements of the quality of leadership and decision-making at many levels among politicians, nobles, patricians, village mayors, diplomats and soldiers. The options for action, seeking advantage and assuring self-preservation can be evaluated, given a person's view of the world, without falling into the trap of either monocausal or pluralistic explanations – but only if the religious and territorial mentalities of the times are used as a basis.

An economic explanation has become the most inviting interpretation from a twentieth-century point of view. The links are all the more tempting in view of marxist historicism, two world wars, Versailles, the Cold War and ideological split, the Chinese war-lord period, Vietnam and its thirty years war, economic unevenness and the Depression. One might think of early seventeenth-century equivalents – in confessional conflicts, the debasement of 1621–2, the Bohemian, Dutch, Danish, Imperialist, Swedish and French phases of war, the Edict of Restitution and the peace treaties of Prague (1635) and Westphalia. Yet the economic explanation can offer more than that. No one would have denied that economic production was the basis of material life, and without it no social organization, diplomacy, war or peace could be envisaged. What will always remain contentious is the combination of material and ideological circumstances to produce not necessary but sufficient explanations of thought and action, saying what occurred, placing it in the context of past and future, which is at the heart of the question 'why'. The notorious difficulty of sorting out this question especially for the first half of the seventeenth century can be seen in the way in which a materialist and marxist historiography emerged in the 1950s, which produced the view of a 'general crisis' of European society in the 1640s without including its geographical centre-piece, namely the Germany of the Thirty Years War. The 'general crisis' debate probably failed in the late 1960s because of this omission, although the main problems are still in economics.

Were the German territorial, town and village economies at the centre or at the periphery of European production, marketing and consumption? To what extent did shifts in international trade, away from northern Italy, south Netherlands and Upper Germany towards maritime France, Britain and Holland, affect internal regional trade, especially in the German hinterlands beyond the Rhine and North Sea coast? If Amsterdam controlled Polish Vistula grain, then it is equally the case that cities like Nuremberg controlled Hungarian cattle exports. East Elbian latifundia (large estate) farming was shot through with exceptions of which the peasant agriculture of Saxony was the leading example. Although the Hanseatic League declined in Lübeck and along the southwest Baltic coast, it successfully regrouped around Hamburg, Bremen and German North Sea outlets.

Although the German territories increased their population in the second half of the sixteenth century, there was a slowing down of economic growth when compared with the Atlantic region. In Upper Germany mining, textiles, long-distance trade and banking suffered contraction and the first great bankruptcies coincided with the coinage debasement and collapse of business confidence of the early 1620s. Between 1550 and 1620 many German territories were adjusted to harder terms of trade, higher inflation, increased population and greater underemployment. Internal trade was being consolidated and the future was seen to lie in greater exploitation of the immediate hinterland between Hamburg and Prague along the Elbe and Vlatava, in Silesia and West Prussia along the Oder and Vistula, across the Carpathians into industrial north Bohemia and Slovakia, and onto the pastures of Hungary. This east-central European economy was handled by German urban centres like Leipzig and Nuremberg on its western periphery, and it was still being consolidated up to 1650. From the 1620s war brought guaranteed prices, ready markets and new opportunities for industry and manufacture, but they could be exploited only where the rationale of seventeenth-century mainland warfare allowed reorganization of production. The war undoubtedly speeded up turnover of goods and services. In winter and springtime billeted armies introduced systems of tribute-barter-tribute called *Kriegskontribution*, which the Spaniards probably pioneered in the Palatinate in 1620 and which was effectively exploited by all subsequent military commanders, above all Tilly, Wallenstein and the Swedes.

Traditional rents and taxes were channelled into war chests, leading to massive new litigation with the revival of federal cameral tribunal activities, especially in the 1630s. Army paymasters and regimental treasurers were the new power over territorial officials, often replacing for a while the authority of local nobles and patricians over collection, or at least over spending of rents and taxes. Compromise was usually reached between traditional civic and new military officials by increasing levels of extraordinary taxation, and widening its net socially upwards as well as downwards. Once increased, taxes, whether direct or indirect, were never decreased despite the coming of peace in the 1650s. Unevenness and shifts in production caused by the vicissitudes of campaigning and billeting armies combined with religious conflict to produce great numbers of temporary exiles who often sought refuge in overcrowded and diseased towns and forts. In certain localities, above all on a diagonal line right through Germany from the north-east to the south-west, from Mecklenburg and Pomerania, through parts of Brandenburg, Thuringia, Saxony, Franconia, Palatinate, Upper Rhine and Swabia, economic organization collapsed, although spectacular calamities like the Sack of Magdeburg in 1631 were great exceptions. This did not minimize the fear that they put into people's hearts.

Yet unevenness and shift, migration of workforces often with capital resources and manufacturing skills benefited many regions, especially parts of the Lower Rhineland, Lower Saxony and Slesvig-Holstein. Agriculture, the primary sector, was run at low capital cost and usually recovered swiftly with the organization of seed-corn from the nearest town or fort, of protected field-work and of safer access to markets and mills. Admittedly, this was a complicated, oft-renewed and destroyed task, as the chronicle of Abbot Friesenegger, at Andechs between Munich and Augsburg, shows. Since wartime massively increased the demand for foodstuffs, it offered quick profits as well as dire insecurity right in the wake of any army, whether friendly or hostile, fighting, marching or billeting. However, all armies lived on the land and in the eyes of the local inhabitants no army was friendly. In the winter of 1633–4, after experiencing the billets of Spaniards and Italians ostensibly helping Elector Maximilian of Bavaria to rid south-east Germany of the Swedes, Abbot Friesenegger reported that his Counter-Reformation Catholic villagers were even murmuring that they would have preferred the troops of their Protestant enemy.

People learned to live with the war and developed a mentality of *Kriegsraison*, which was a machiavellian pragmatism of raison d'état, entailing massive increases in taxation and communications. It increased the prerogative power of officials dealing with emergencies on the spot, who ultimately became responsible as commissioners to their territorial ruler or government. *Kriegsraison* demanded swift reconstruction of devastated areas, reconsolidation of agriculture, high taxes, quick turnover at market and volatile labour relations. It demanded the consolation of religion, in the form of a wrathful God for most and Fortuna the fickle for some others: billets, fire and plague were becoming the natural lieutenants of the overall, ever-present enemy – far more sinister than Mansfeld, Tilly, Spinola, Wallenstein, Gustavus Adolphus, Bernhard of Saxe-Weimar, Horn, Königsmarck and de Werth – namely contagious diseases, the weather and the poor productivity of crops and cattle.

What is meant by 'crisis'? In the early seventeenth century it was becoming a political word on loan from medical science. Just as an unwell person reached a point in his contagion, after which he either died or recovered but did not for long stay suspended between the two, so, by analogy with the human body, the body-politic when afflicted by war, pestilence or rebellion either recovered or disintegrated. As a starting point this crude organic theory of state may help us to come closer again to the mentality of the period.

The purpose of this selection of documents is to draw attention to this crisis among sections of early modern German government, economy and society, using religious conflict as the ideological superstructure and economic development as the material basis for the choices made. This rough approach is deemed necessary since no thematically useful collection of documents on the Thirty Years War exists in any language, although the work of J. Polišenský from the Czech archives comes closest to filling this gap at an erudite and linguistically complex level of scholarship. The aim of this collection is to provide documents in translation for further discussion and also support for the general studies of the period which are outlined at the beginning of the select bibliography (p. 101). The documents are grouped under sections on background and social impact. The first part sets the scene by including a number of more formal documents and the second part is more interpretive. Both parts concentrate on the problems of religion, economics, and the politics of *Kriegsraison*. The reader may ponder the questions: To what extent did wartime shape German society? Where, if at all, would one place the Germany of the Thirty Years War in the seventeenth-century crisis? To what extent did the war hasten absolutism and militarism, and how did it alter the German public mind both temporarily and permanently? Did the war clearly begin to turn German patriotism into German nationalism?

The documents seek to stress in particular the impact of wartime on various sections of the early modern German population, in the open country as well as behind the walls and earthworks of towns and forts, questioning to what extent the Thirty Years War was a period of total war and of war propaganda, war journalism and war economy. The four social groupings used are peasants and soldiers, townsmen, nobles and clergy, military commanders, and rulers and diplomats. The immediate impact on many of them concerned recruitment, billeting, *Brandschatzung* (arbitrary war taxes), and life under occupation with its protection (*salva guardia*), brief flight, return home and its consequences. The longer-term impact included psychological and material damage caused by food shortage, famine and fire, migration and exile and, the biggest killers of all, overcrowding, contaminated water and contagious diseases.

The question is not so much 'why did hostilities last so long?' (especially after the failure of an all-German peace initiative in 1635) but rather 'why were the diplomats of Europe so successful in concluding peace between 1643–8?' (a peace which then effectively took another five years to implement). The Nuremberg executive of 1649–50 demobilized Swedes and Imperialists by using millions of talers in federal taxes, and the Imperial assembly of 1653–4 unilaterally restricted levels of war-debt repayment, saving many German territories and urban centres from impossibly high interest rates or even bankruptcy. What qualities had the generation of politicians and administrators in power during the 1640s and 1650s that the previous generation of the 1620s and 1630s seem to have lacked (although all the conventional 'heroes' come from the earlier period)? What moral factors dictated events and what material necessities shaped both?

PART I BACKGROUND

I Politics and the constitution

In 1555 the German Imperial constitution was reformed in such a way as to produce political toleration of territorial authorities who adhered to the Augsburg Confession of 1530 and who had become Lutheran before 1552 (1). The majority of territorial authorities remained Catholic, and after the introduction of the Tridentine reforms towards the end of the sixteenth century, constitutional cooperation became increasingly difficult. On the Protestant side Lutheran moderates began to disagree with Calvinist activists who were not recognized constitutionally. In the 1590s Imperial federal taxes were still raised to combat the Turks, which produced some unity and cohesion in German politics. Yet a decade later home affairs predominated and, after initial refusals to pay taxes in support of Imperial federal instances of government, law and order, three antagonistic 'parties' began to emerge. They were the Counter-Reformation Catholics under the mutual rivals, Maximilian of Bavaria and Ferdinand of Styria (the future Habsburg ruler of Bohemia and Emperor of Germany from 1619); the Lutheran moderates under Elector John George of Saxony; and the Calvinists led by politicians from Heidelberg, especially under the young Frederick of the Palatinate (the 'Winter King' of the Bohemian rebel Estates).

The Protestant radicals formed their own union of defence under Palatinate leadership in 1608 and ten years later seized their chance to wrest Bohemia from the Catholic Habsburgs (2, 4). The Catholic militants replied in 1609 with a league under Bavarian leadership which above all included all the remaining ecclesiastical territories, headed by the bishop of Würzburg (3). Ten years later Bavaria and Austria agreed to drive the Protestants out of Bohemia (5). In the warfare of the 1620s the Catholics were overwhelmingly successful, but Ferdinand II's Edict of Restitution contained the threat of despotism which alienated many German dynastic territories: they felt that their autonomy within the Imperial federal constitution would next be threatened if the Habsburgs continued to re-Catholicize and expel fellow Protestant rulers such as those of

Mecklenburg, parts of the Lower Saxon Guelph, parts of the Hessian, and parts of the Palatine Wittelsbach dynastic complexes (6).

Swedish intervention was regarded as essential to the survival of moderate, let alone militant Protestantism, and it was reaffirmed by the Heilbronn Confederation in 1633, despite the death of King Gustavus Adolphus at Lützen half a year previously (7). Yet the Heilbronn Confederation was due to the skill of Swedish chancellor, Axel Oxenstierna, rather than to Protestant fervour, and Saxony and Brandenburg reached accord with the Emperor over the terms of an all-German territorial peace at Prague in 1635 (8). The rest of the war years were effectively spent in accommodating to the terms demanded by the great powers outside the German territorial political scene, above all by France, Sweden, and the Spanish and Austrian Habsburgs, with the involvement of the Dutch, the south Netherlands, northern Italy and the Papacy, some helping some hindering the long-drawn out proceedings towards peace during most of the 1640s (9–11).

1 The Religious Peace of Augsburg, 1555

15   In order to bring peace into the Holy Empire of the Germanic Nation between the Roman Imperial Majesty and the Electors, Princes and Estates, let neither His Imperial Majesty nor the Electors, Princes, etc., do any violence or harm to any estate of the empire on account of the Augsburg Confession, but let them enjoy their religious belief, liturgy and ceremonies as well as their estates and other rights and privileges in peace; and complete religious peace shall be obtained only by Christian means of amity, or under threat of the punishment of the Imperial ban.

16   Likewise the Estates espousing the Augsburg Confession shall let all the Estates and Princes who cling to the old religion live in absolute peace and in the enjoyment of all their estates, rights and privileges.

17   However, all such as do not belong to the two above named religions shall not be included in the present peace but be totally excluded from it.

18   And since it has proved to be a matter of great dispute what was to happen with the bishoprics, priories and other ecclesiastical benefices of such Catholic priests who would in course of time abandon the old religion, we have in virtue of the powers of Roman Emperors ordained as follows: where an archbishop, bishop or prelate or any other priest of our old religion shall abandon the same, his archbishopric, bishopric, prelacy and other benefices together with all their income and revenues which he has so far possessed, shall be abandoned by him without any further

objection or delay. The chapter and such as are entitled to it by common law or the custom of the place shall elect a person espousing the old religion who may enter on the possession and enjoyment of all the rights and incomes of the place without any further hindrance and without prejudging any ultimate amicable transaction of religion.

19 Some of the abbeys, monasteries and other ecclesiastical estates having been confiscated and turned into churches, schools and charitable institutions, it is herewith ordained that such estates which their original owners had not possessed at the time of the Treaty of Passau [1552] shall be comprised in the present treaty of peace.

20 The ecclesiastical jurisdiction over the Augsburg Confession, dogma, appointment of ministers, church ordinances, and ministeries hitherto practised (but apart from all the rights of the Electors, Princes and Estates colleges and monasteries to taxes in money or tithes) shall from now cease and the Augsburg Confession shall be left to the free and untrammelled enjoyment of their religion, ceremonies, appointment of ministers, as is stated in a subsequent separate article, until the final transaction of religion will take place.

23 No Estate shall try to persuade the subjects of other Estates to abandon their religion nor protect them against their own magistrates. Such as had from olden times the rights of patronage are not included in the present article.

24 In case our subjects whether belonging to the old religion or the Augsburg Confession should intend leaving their homes with their wives and children in order to settle in another place, they shall be hindered neither in the sale of their estates after due payment of the local taxes nor injured in their honour.

E. Reich (ed.), Select Documents (London, 1905), 230–32

2 The Protestant Union, 1608

The Union (*Verain*) between the Palatinate, Electoral Brandenburg, Württemberg, Ansbach and Baden, made at Auhausen in Franconia.

In view of the urgent necessity, we, the undersigned Electors and Estates of the Holy Empire, much less to damage but much more to strengthen and uphold peace and unity in the Holy Empire, as dedicated and obedient Estates of the Empire of the German Nation, our beloved fatherland, in order to advance the common well-being, our land and people and also those Estates who will in future join us to further peace, order and protection in the name of God the Almighty, have one and all reached the present amicable and confidential agreement which we acknowledge by virtue of this letter, as follows:

1   That each member shall keep good faith with the other and their heirs, land and people, and that no one shall enter any other alliance; also that no Estate, jurisdiction, territory or subjects shall damage, fight or in any way harm another Estate, nor break the laws of the Imperial constitution, nor give aid in any manner if such a break should occur;

2   That we and all our heirs who are in this Union shall keep a secret correspondence effectively to inform each other of all dangerous and offensive affairs which may threaten each other's heirs, land and people, and to this purpose each will keep in good contact with the other.

3   Whenever important matters arise that concern the well-being of us all, we and our heirs, for the duration of this Union will help each other with faithful advice in order to uphold each and every one as far as possible unharmed in his Estate and territory. . . . .

4   It is our wish that in matters concerning the liberties and high jurisdictions of the German Electors and Estates, as also of the Protestant [*Evangelische*] Estates' grievances as presented at the last Imperial assembly concerning infringements of those selfsame rights, freedoms and laws of the Empire, these shall all be presented and pressed at subsequent Imperial and Imperial Circle assemblies, and not merely left to secret correspondence with each other. We also agree to try to influence other Protestant Estates [i.e. Saxony] towards an understanding with us.

5   We also agree that this secret union shall not affect our disagreement on several points of religion, but that notwithstanding these, we have agreed to support each other. No member is to allow an attack on any other in books or through the pulpit, nor give cause for any breach of the peace, whilst at the same time leaving untouched the theologian's right of disputation to affirm the Word of God.

6   If one or other of us is attacked . . . the remaining members of the Union shall immediately come to his aid with all the resources of the Union, as necessity may demand, and as set out in the detailed agreement. . . .

Should any member of the Union inherit or enlarge his territory in the future, then the new land and people will pay a contribution proportional to the federal tax schedule [*Reichsmatricul*] according to the needs of the treasury [*Cassa*] of the Union.

H. H. Hofmann (ed.), *Quellen zum Verfas-sungsorganismus, 1495–1815* (Darmstadt, 1976), 151–3

3 The Catholic League, 1609

The League was made between Bavaria, Würzburg and most of the ecclesiastical rulers in the Empire at Munich in July 1609, and was agreed for nine years in the first instance. The commander of the League was Duke Maximilian of Bavaria. He had already 'disciplined' the Protestants of the Imperial city of Donauwörth on his own initiative in 1607.

We agree that no one of us shall aid, help or succour in any manner whatsoever each other's enemy, but instead give advice and real aid to prosecute such an enemy just as if he were one's own enemy. And any such action is to be reported immediately to the commander of the League who will be requested to provide advice and aid.

Since we live in these dangerous and warlike times as well within as outwith the Empire, the members of the League are to exchange information of any clandestine or open recruiting of soldiers, armaments or similar activities that come to their notice, in order to warn all their fellow members in good faith, and to inform the commander of the League by letter, or where the matter is too dangerous for that, by word of mouth. The commander of the League will then know what action to take and he may decide to call an assembly of the League [*bundstag*] or arrange the necessary military action [*bundshilf*] through consultation with his subordinates and other military advisers appointed by the League.

Should anyone among our federated ranks be attacked by anyone acting against the land and religious peace of the Empire, its constitutions and Imperial assembly laws, and should all attempts at legal and peaceful mediation be of no avail, then the aggrieved party is to inform the commander of the League, who will immediately inform the aggressor to desist, inviting him to accept the mediation of the League. But if a member of the League himself does not abide by the laws of the Empire, the League is not bound to support that member in his specific conflict. . . .

If one or other member of the League is directly attacked, all the other members are by virtue of this agreement bound to come to his rescue, but the attacked member shall have no right to make a separate peace with his attacker. Instead he shall negotiate peace to the full satisfaction of all his fellow members in the League.

Henceforth every Estate and member of the League shall undertake to keep his land and people in good military preparedness, in order to be ready to defend himself against any disadvantage or damage, and should such disadvantage and damage [*schaden und nachtail*] nevertheless occur, all the members of the League shall be committed to help and to compensate him for his losses.

Hofmann, 153–6

4   The Defenestration of Prague, 1618

A Catholic Habsburg version.

Throughout the Holy Roman Empire, in all kingdoms and principalities of Christendom it has been seen as wicked and punishable that certain persons of Bohemian origin from the two higher Estates of the Land have perpetrated such a shameful evil act the like of which was unknown in the annals of the world, namely that two viceroys of His Royal Majesty [Ferdinand] and highest officers of the Land of Bohemia have been cast mercilessly out of the window into a deep valley. . . .

Four members of the Estate of Lords and one knight, namely Wilhelm von Lobkowitz, Albrecht Smiřicky, Ulrich Kinsky, Litwin von Ričan and Paul Kaplíř, forcibly laid hands on the count of Martinitz, held him down and led him to the opened window whilst shouting: 'Now we will take our just revenge on our religious enemies.' The two counts thought that they would be led out of the chancellery and placed under arrest, but when Martinitz understood the nature of his impending death, he loudly called out: 'Since I must now die for God, His Holy Catholic Faith and His Royal Majesty, I will put up with anything but only allow me to see my confessor so that I can confess my sins.' Those gentlemen who were present only gave him the following reply: 'We will now send a villainous Jesuit to join you.' Whilst Count Martinitz was highly troubled at this and sincerely beginning to repent his sins, praying: 'Jesus, you Son of the living God, have mercy on me, Mother of God take pity on me', the above named persons lifted him off the ground and cast him together with sword and dagger but without hat, which one of them had torn out of his hand, head first out of the window into the depth of the castle moat.

As he fell, he called out the names of Jesus and Mary, and he landed so gently on the ground that it was as if he were merely sitting down so that his plea to the Virgin Mary and the protection of God during his terrible fall saved him from all harm despite his corpulent body. Several devout and trustworthy people have also affirmed that whilst going with the procession over the bridge they saw the most serene Virgin Mary catch the gentleman in the air with her cloak and carry him to earth. Count Martinitz did not see this himself but during the fall he had a vision that heaven was opening and that God wished to take him up to everlasting happiness.

H. Schulz (ed.), *Der dreissigjährige Krieg* I
(Leipzig, 1917), 31–2

5   The Treaty of Munich, 1619

The Treaty united Austria and the Catholic League under Bavarian leadership in war against the Bohemian rebels and the Protestant Union. Maximilian's price was control of the government and revenues of Upper Austria until Emperor Ferdinand II had paid all his ensuing war debts to Bavaria, and also transfer of the highest secular Electoral dignity in the Empire from the Palatinate to Bavaria which was forced through by Imperial decree in 1620.

On behalf of the Holy Roman Emperor, King of Hungary and Bohemia, and on behalf of the German ecclesiastical Electors, His Grace, Duke Maximilian of Bavaria, has been requested for the common good of all of us to take over full command of the Catholic defences to which the high Catholic Estates of the Empire, His Imperial Majesty, his dynasty and the endangered lands have been constrained for their own preservation to agree. From this task His Grace, the Duke of Bavaria, has not dissented, as a sign of his friendly feelings towards His Imperial Majesty, towards His Royal Highness in Spain, and towards the whole praiseworthy House of Austria, to protect the Catholic religion and all the Estates of the Empire loyal to it.

His Grace, the Duke of Bavaria, is granted free and absolute command over the Catholic system of defence including recruitment and movement of the troops whom he will lead in the name of the Almighty, but on the following express condition. For as long as they are under threat, His Grace, the Duke of Bavaria, shall have the full support with money and troops of all the Catholic Estates as well as of His Imperial Highness, and that this aid in money and troops will be forthcoming for as long as His Grace, the Duke of Bavaria, as supreme commander, deems necessary. And furthermore, His Imperial Majesty shall not hinder His Grace, the Duke of Bavaria, in any manner whatsoever from exercising absolute and total command.

In return, His Grace, the Duke of Bavaria, will to the best of his ability make open war on all the enemies of His Imperial Majesty, including any of the Estates of the Protestant Union who subsequently become his enemies. It is expressly stated that His Imperial Majesty will refrain from any negotiations, suspension of hostilities or conclusion of truce or peace with the enemies without prior knowledge, consent and inclusion of His

Grace, the Duke of Bavaria. His Imperial Majesty also undertakes to carry the costs of war and of war damage as outlined in greater detail below. . . . And His Grace, the Duke of Bavaria, undertakes to support His Imperial Majesty in like manner.

Schulz I, 32–5

6   The Edict of Restitution, 1629

We, Ferdinand, by the grace of God, Holy Roman Emperor, etc., are determined for the realization both of the religious and profane peace to despatch our Imperial commissioners into the Empire; to reclaim all the archbishoprics, bishoprics, prelacies, monasteries, hospitals and endowments which the Catholics had possessed at the time of the Treaty of Passau [1552] and of which they have been illegally deprived; and to put into all these Catholic foundations duly qualified persons so that each may get his proper due. We herewith declare that the Religious Peace [of 1555] refers only to the Augsburg Confession as it was submitted to our ancestor Emperor Charles V on 25 June 1530; and that all other doctrines and sects, whatever names they may have, not included in the Peace are forbidden and cannot be tolerated. We therefore command to all and everybody under punishment of the religious and the land ban that they shall at once cease opposing our ordinance and carry it out in their lands and territories and also assist our commissioners. Such as hold the archbishoprics and bishoprics, prelacies, monasteries, hospitals, etc., shall forthwith return them to our Imperial commissioners with all their appurtenances. Should they not carry out this behest they will not only expose themselves to the Imperial ban and to the immediate loss of all their privileges and rights without any further sentence or condemnation, but to the inevitable real execution of that order and be distrained by force.

Reich, 234–5

7   The Confederation of Heilbronn, 1633

The confederation was between the crown of Sweden and the Protestant Estates of the four Upper Circles of the Empire.

First, the Princes and Estates who have met here with the Crown of Sweden under the guidance of the Royal Swedish Chancellor [Axel Oxenstierna] freely agree to join together in alliance [*Confoederieren*] and give each other mutual aid in order that the freedom of Germany [*Teutsche Libertät*] and also observance of the statutes and laws of the Holy Roman

Empire shall once again be observed, and that the restitution of the Protestant Estates' rights in matters secular and religious shall be kept in a safely concluded peace. Furthermore, the Crown of Sweden is to have compensation [*satisfaction*], and all the separate alliances that the Crown of Sweden has made with individual Princes and Estates in the four Upper Circles of the Empire [that is, the Protestant Estates of the Electoral-Rhenish, Franconian, Swabian and Upper-Rhenish Circles] shall continue to be upheld in all points and not be suspended but rather extended. Such separate alliances shall instead enhance the strength of this confederation by impressing on every member the importance of and need for each and every one's full contributions to be rendered to it.

Second, because an effective wartime alliance needs leadership, so the Crown of Sweden under the guidance of Chancellor Oxenstierna has agreed to accept the same on the demand of the assembled confederates. . . .

Third, that to help the Chancellor, a council of well qualified persons shall be appointed to organize the forces of the confederates and of the Circles. . . .

Fourth, no confederate member shall enter into any separate negotiations with the enemy unless it is with the prior consent of the Chancellor and fellow confederates. All such matters shall be brought before the confederate council and the assemblies of the Circles.

Fifth, if any confederate tries to make his own policy [*gefaehrlicher Practicen*] such as becoming neutral, then when he is under threat or attack from the enemy, he shall not receive aid from the confederation. . . .

Sixth, it is agreed that for the duration of the war and until an agreed peace can be achieved, the confederates in the four Circles shall keep armies properly supplied with money, food, ammunition and artillery [*Gelt, Viures, ammunition vnnd Artillerie*]. . . .

Seventh, in order that the war may be waged more effectively, strict army discipline shall be enforced and all excesses are to be prevented. The troops are to be regularly supplied with field treasuries and depots.

Eighth, the Chancellor has promised to consult his council and provide military reforms, restrain the regiments that have caused trouble and restore discipline in order that commerce may flourish once more among the ordinary people who will then be able to earn their living again. The Estates shall have their powers of jurisdiction and police restored and all extortions, billets and route marches shall henceforth be strictly supervised. As far as possible the local authorities shall have power to assign billets and all the Estates shall have supervisory power over the ways and means of paying the soldiers quartered on them in their localities.

Ninth, the confederates beg the Crown of Sweden to continue to fight for restitution of lands and jurisdictions and to press for compensation from their enemies in the Empire. . . .

Finally, although this confederation has been deemed necessary for the defence of all peace-loving Estates in the Empire, it in no way abrogates the laws of the Holy Roman Empire but instead reaffirms all the rights of the Imperial Estates and their subjects and especially those of the Protestants.

Schulz II, 8–17

8   The Peace of Prague, 1635

Made between the Emperor and Saxony, May 1635.

3   Concerning all the ecclesiastical lands and properties that lay within territorial state jurisdiction and that were already secularized before the agreement at Passau [of 1552] by the Electors and Imperial Estates who are members of the Augsburg Confession [Lutherans], they shall all remain according to the clear letter and direction of the established, highly esteemed religious peace [of 1555].

4   However, concerning the ecclesiastical lands and properties that were territorial states in their own right, and that were secularized before the agreement at Passau, as well as all those ecclesiastical lands and properties that have fallen into the hands of members of the Augsburg Confession after the conclusion of the Passau agreement, whether they lay within territorial state jurisdiction or were territorial states in their own right, we have finally agreed that those Electors and Imperial Estates who held these lands on 12 November 1627, new style, shall have complete and free control of the same for a period of forty years from the date of this concluded agreement. And any authority that has been deprived of such lands since 12 November 1627 shall have them returned, yet without any right to claim costs or damages.

74   To achieve the long-desired pacification of our dear fatherland of the German nation . . . each and every military occupation, recruiting and mustering, war tax and other grievance against the laws of the Empire, with which the Empire has recently been burdened, is in future to cease entirely, and is never to be enforced again.

75   In like manner there shall never be another particular military constitution set up within the Empire, be it from the head or members, that goes against the Emperor's coronation oath, the laws of the Empire, and of the Imperial Circles.

76   In no matters, including those agreed in this treaty and above all those concerning the Palatinate affair, shall any armed foreign power be tolerated to come onto German soil, unless it is with the grant, order and permission of the Emperor, and if this should occur then all effort shall be directed against it.

77   Furthermore, with the establishment and publication of this peace all unions, leagues, federations and suchlike agreements, as well as all oaths and duties sworn on the same, are totally null and void, and only the Imperial and Circle laws shall be kept, although this shall in no way imply any dissolution of the college of Electors.

Hofmann, 162–4

9–10   The Peace of Westphalia, 1648

9   The Treaty of Osnabrück, Westphalia, 1648

Article 5: from paragraphs 1 and 30

The Religious Peace of 1555, as it was later confirmed . . . by various Imperial diets, shall, in all its articles entered into and concluded by the unanimous consent of the Emperor, Electors, Princes and Estates of both religions, be confirmed and observed fully and without infringement. . . . In all matters there shall be an exact and mutual equality between all the Electors, Princes and states of either religion, as far as agrees with the constitution of the realm, the Imperial decrees, and the present treaty; so that what is right for one side shall also be right for the other; all violence and other contrary proceedings being herewith between the two sides for ever prohibited. . . .

Whereas all immediate states enjoy, together with their territorial rights and sovereignty as hitherto used throughout the Empire, also the right of reforming the practice of religion; and whereas in the Religious Peace the privilege of emigration was conceded to the subjects of such states if they dissented from the religion of their territorial lord; and whereas later, for the better preserving of greater concord among the states, it was agreed that no one should seduce another's subjects to his religion, or for that reason make any undertaking of defence or protection, or come to their aid for any reason; it is now agreed that all these be fully observed by the states of either religion, and that no state shall be hindered in the rights in matters of religion, which belong to it by reason of its territorial independence and sovereignty.

Article 7: from paragraphs 1 and 2

It is agreed by the unanimous consent of His Imperial Majesty and all the

Estates of the Empire that whatever rights and benefits are conferred upon the states and subjects attached to the Catholic and Augsburg [Lutheran] faiths, either by the constitutions of the Empire, or by the Religious Peace and this public treaty . . . shall also apply to those who are called reformed [Calvinists]. . . . Beyond the religions mentioned above, none shall be received or tolerated in the Holy Empire.

G. R. Elton (ed.), *Renaissance and Reformation,
1300–1648* (New York, 1968),249

10 Mazarin's assessment of the peace, 1648

Letter of Cardinal Mazarin to the French envoy, Servien, October 1648.

It might perhaps have been more useful for achieving a general peace if the war could have been pursued a little longer in Germany, instead of our haste to find an accommodation as we have now done. Yet this would have implied that we were in a position to prolong negotiations when instead there was the threat that Sweden might have betrayed us and acted on her own urgent desire to conclude hostilities. The fear of such an unpleasant event overrode all other considerations. I think that the fear of total collapse by the Emperor which, considering his pathetic situation was unavoidably imminent, may have been enough to invite sympathy from the Spaniards, cause them somewhat to soften their harsh stand, and protect him from such a blow. Whereas now they consider him to be secured by the conclusion of peace, despite the conditions, which are quite harsh to him, and they take no more notice of him, nor do they seem to worry about his position, which may otherwise have been a more serious reason for bringing them to conclude peace. We can be quite sure that the greatest aid to the Emperor has now come from us in that we forced him into making peace, for otherwise his total ruin would have been inevitable.

Furthermore, I gather from a reliable source that the Emperor – whether to soften the blow of leaving the Spaniards, to which he is now committed, or whether he really intends to make use of it, as he has let it be known – has assured the king of Spain through the archduke that all that he has done has only occurred in order to deflect the full force of destruction that almost threatened to engulf him, and that this peace is certainly damaging in its hard terms, but that given the situation under which it was concluded, it is very advantageous. A great number of fortified places and lands have been returned to him, which he had already lost, giving him the opportunity to save the rest, which under other circumstances would have been subject to the greatest danger. Since he has now deflected such a powerful blow and has got his breath back somewhat, he is ready at any time to take up the war again, whenever he chooses. For this there would certainly be no lack of pretext, if only he could find the necessary means for his disposal.

L. Bäte (ed.), *Der Friede in Osnabrück* (Oldenburg, 1948), 147

11   Demobilization, 1649–50

As seen by a peasant craftsman near Ulm.

This year, 1649, is a joyful year of celebration but even though peace was made in 1648, it has not been implemented fully. Yet God alone be praised for having made peace in our Germany and throughout the [Holy] Roman Empire among the Emperor, Swedes, French and all kings, princes, counts and cities, villages, hamlets, farms and cottages, whether rich or poor, young or old, woman and man, wife and child; in short, the dear cattle and horses and all will benefit from peacetime and look forward to it. Yes, and also the dear fields which have long been neglected and lain fallow will once again be ploughed and sown, in order that we miserable children of man can nourish ourselves and heal our sorrows. Also, that we may once more make our living in crafts and manufactures in order to pay for the riders billeted on us, pay the peace tax [for demobilization], and finally bring to an end this great succession of burdens and demands.

On 6 January [1649] a regiment of Swedish riders was billeted in all the hamlets of our Ulm district, and we had to pay a lot of money [each horseman was granted 6 batzen, that is, 24 kreuzer per day, or its preferred equivalent in goods].

Once peace was concluded at Münster and approved by everyone, a date was set by those assembled there to meet again within a year at Nuremberg, where the terms of peace were finally worked out with unanimity [*Friedensexekutionshauptabschied*, 16 June 1650].

Once those who were in charge had reached agreement among themselves as how best to demobilize their regiments and avoid outbreaks in the Empire of any untoward mutinies which could have led to robbery, plunder and other unpleasantness, since there were very many evil and daring scoundrels, as is usual, among the soldiers, the actual carrying out of these orders took a very long time. In the meantime we continued to pay our demobilization taxes month after month, week after week and day after day. But God be praised, at last the day arrived in our land of Ulm when our regiment was mustered and marched out in good peace and without any further damage. This occurred on 11 October in the week of the Holzkirch consecration. . . .

The seven Imperial Circles of the Empire were ordered to pay the Swedes and their armies five million reichstalers in three instalments. The first instalment was 1,800,000 reichstalers in cash. The Electoral Rhenish and Upper Rhenish Circles were ordered to pay their contributions to Frankfurt-am-Main. The Upper Saxon Circle was to pay to Leipzig or Brunswick; the Franconian Circle at Nuremberg; the Swabian Circle at Ulm; the Westphalian Circle at Bremen or Münster and the Lower Saxon Circle at Hamburg. And everyone had to meet and work out his share of the 1,800,000 reichstalers in assessment. And that is what they concluded at Nuremberg.

On 24 August [1650] on St Bartholomew's Day, a thanksgiving feast was given in Ulm and all the villages around the city. There were sermons, songs, prayers and holy communion was joyfully celebrated, since all the garrisons of troops had now left their billets and towns, and we now had full and total peace by the grace of God Almighty. And the following fine prayer was composed and spoken from all the pulpits especially for the occasion.

We thank you, Dear Lord, that you have given us peace after years of suffering turmoil and war, and that you have granted our pleas. We thank you for pulling us like a brand out of the fire, allowing us to rescue our life almost as if it were itself war booty. Oh Merciful Father, how can we atone sufficiently for this great kindness that you have so graciously deigned to grant us, who are not worthy to raise our eyes to you in Heaven, in our prayers and in giving us what we have asked from you.

Oh Lord, you have indeed treated us with mercy that our city and lands, which had previously been full of fear and horror, are now full of joy and happiness. We beseech you, who has saved us from the sword, to mercifully let our corn grow again, that we may multiply and prosper once more. That we may live securely, rebuild, Dear Lord, a fig-tree and a vine-stock in each of us that our destroyed and torn down dwellings may again be built up, and that the ravaged land may be ploughed once more, in order that all people shall know that you are the Lord who has rebuilt what was destroyed, and replanted what was ravaged.

Oh God, the lover of peace, grant us henceforth permanent peace and leave our boundaries and houses in calm and peace that the voice of the war messenger does not frighten us, and that the man-of-war does not touch us.

Hans Heberle, *Zeytregister (1618–72). Der Dreissigjährige Krieg in zeitgenössischer Darstellung*, edited by G. Zillhardt (Ulm, 1975), 226–7, 235–7

II Economics and the military system

It is unlikely that the outbreak of hostilities in Bohemia and in the two parts of the Palatinate near Bohemia and in the Rhineland were the direct cause of the great inflation of 1621–4 which affected most parts of Germany. Hostilities had strictly local impact and army leaders were quick to pioneer a system of requisition, add it to existing tax burdens and insist on priority in payment. Yet the coinage debasement, destruction of business confidence and rise in prices of the years 1621–4 would probably have occurred whether there had been a war or not: the severely deflationary economic policies of the Empire as operated through most of its regional Imperial Circles since the late 1550s no longer, by the early seventeenth century, corresponded to the realities of German trade performance in the wider world (12, 13).

The Spanish economy was also under attack. Despite successes on land, in the Rhineland and even along the south Baltic coast during the 1620s, the rebellious Dutch closed the Channel, North Sea and south Netherlands ports and threatened transatlantic communications (18). The brief rise of neutral Dover as an entrepôt resulted in shipping figures almost on a par with those of Hamburg (19, 20). Disruption and redeployment of sea trade produced naval strategies that were a counterpart of *Kriegskontribution* and the military system on land.

The military crisis was just as much a naval crisis, especially among the coastal towns and villages of the south Baltic. Pillage was the natural outcome of *Kriegskontribution*, when army discipline broke down owing to a great many factors such as lack of surplus in the primary sector of production, actual hostilities, disease, poor communications, weather and the deficiencies of local administration and leadership (21–4). The effects of a few, well publicized, notorious actions have provided the sources for the traditional historical interpretation of the Thirty Years War, and they are locally important; yet there is always a danger in oversimplifying and overgeneralizing these effects (Maps 1 and 2, 36).

Did the war years produce their own, unique economic system? In the short term, probably yes; in the long term, probably no. What was the price that civilians paid for survival? Military discipline was certainly tightened time and again – a necessity as Axel Oxenstierna admitted in 1633 (7) – although such conscientiousness had not prevented spectacular failures (22). The technological level of warfare was not sufficiently powerful to threaten the traditional preindustrial system of low-investment agriculture, marketing and urban manufacture (16, 17), nor to develop it markedly, and Wallenstein's military-industrial enterprises remained very much localized and exceptional. Although standing armies emerged out of years of mercenary warfare by mid-century, preindustrial capitalism remained essentially controlled by town councils, nobles, dynasties and traditional, civilian elites.

Agriculture usually recovered very swiftly and the *longue durée* of the harvest cycle eventually forced most soldiers back to the land. The fruitfulness of the growth cycle assured quick recovery sometimes well before the formal peace years of the 1650s, and even pastors exiled, often briefly, by priests, and vice versa, could survive quite comfortably (25, 26).

12 The great inflation, 1621–4

The experience of a cobbler near Ulm (see above, p. xvi for a note on coinage).

In the year 1621 the haggling started and everyone wanted to get rich overnight. Some ran this way and some that way until they had exported all the good coin in return for bringing into our territory debased, loose change which was nothing more than copper and brass. All the territories were ruined by it and prices shot up especially in 1622–4, creating chaotic conditions the like of which have never been seen since the beginning of the world. In this year [1621] corn reached 20 gulden and rye sold at 15. In short, everything was sold at a premium. It was also the year that Spinola conquered the Rhineland Palatinate. . . .

I will not turn to describing the inflationary situation during 1622. A great number of unrecognizable coins circulated since all emperors and kings, princes and lords, counts and noblemen, towns and markets, tinkers and wayfarers minted and obtained permission to mint their own coins. There were so many different sorts of coin that you had to be good at languages and clear-sighted enough to read all the inscriptions. It was light, counterfeit money with no substance. To start with it looked brand new like silver but in three to eight weeks it was shabby and red like copper, that is, excluding taler coins and old money. Since the money was soon worthless, no one wanted to accept it in payment. That led to chaos everywhere.

The authorities in Ulm as elsewhere finally forbade the tender of all tin and debased metal coins, since widows and orphans and anyone else who used this money would soon have lost all their goods and property, and those fellows who tried to handle this money would soon have paid all their debts however many thousand real talers they owed, thereby swindling their creditors. Within three months anyone who held such money lost more than half to a whole of its starting value. At first 3 betzner were worth 10 kreuzer. Three months later they were down to $7\frac{1}{2}$ kreuzer. They finally sank to 3 kreuzer. The old taler rose to 10 gulden and in some places even reached 12 to 15 gulden, although it then came down to a general 6 gulden.

Small change that had been minted everywhere out of copper into kreuzers and pfennigs was of course a necessity and in popular demand, above all the Ulm coins, where copper kreuzers were worth a half batzen. I myself bought 20 batzen worth of copper since it would have been worth 3 gulden in old money equivalent. But copper coins did not keep their value and they soon dropped to a penny and then a farthing. Finally they became worthless. The end to this cheap money came when no one was prepared to accept anything other than full value talers.

Yet small change was also exported although attempts were made to retain the reichstaler currency. Some bought and sold their goods cheaply with [debased] gulden, and others insisted on [full value] talers only. The poor man was hit hardest when people started to demand payment in talers only, since he had no way of earning them. He starved and suffered great anxiety for wife and child because of the bad coinage since prices were far too high to satisfy the necessities of life. . . .

Clothes and many other goods went up in price very rapidly. A pound of lard cost up to 2 gulden and a measure of salt cost the same . . . meat was 5 batzen to the pound, a measure of wine 20 batzen and beer at 4 batzen. A pair of men's shoes was 7 to 8 gulden and women's boots 9 gulden or more. . . . A peasant's complete outfit that used to cost 8 to 10 gulden now cost 40 to 50 gulden. . . .

[In March 1623] a good horse went for 100 reichstalers and a cow for 100 gulden and more. A calf was 18 gulden, a sheep 15, a goose 3 gulden and a chicken cost 24 batzen. An egg even cost 5 kreuzer. In short, it was extremely expensive and it can not all be told and understood by one person here.

On 12 April corn cost 49 gulden the imen, rye 47, oats 20, barley 36, linseed 32 and pease 28 gulden. . . . And the taler stayed at 6 gulden for nine months before coming down to $1\frac{1}{2}$ gulden again after reaching an all-time high of 22 gulden during 1622. The small-change debased gulden fell to 15 kreuzer . . . and the copper kreuzer was worth a farthing.

Heberle, 96–102, 109–10, 274–5

13–15   Kriegskontribution

13   Bread for Tilly, Lippe, 1623

In July 1623 the chancellery of Count Simon VII of Lippe in eastern Westphalia implored his nobles to send bread for the upkeep of Tilly's Catholic League army.

Since the High-born Count and Lord, Lord Simon, Count and Noble Lord of Lippe, our gracious Lord, has been asked for provisions by General Count of Tilly for the upkeep of His Excellency's army, so His Grace has graciously allowed that as much as is possible be collected up and furthermore be delivered to prevent any untoward incidents in town and country.

Therefore His Grace is graciously inclined towards the worthy nobility of this, His Grace's county, that they each of them in their own districts, produce whatever they can in bread and send it in as quickly as possible to rescue the common welfare [of the county].

Given in the comital chancellery, here [Detmold], 20 July 1623.

Staatsarchiv Detmold, L 11, IV 5a

14   A new agreement between Tilly's army and Lippe, 1630

Short minutes of agreement reached when auditing the accounts of Count von Tilly, recording what was unanimously concluded in Castle Detmold on 10 March 1630.

1   His Excellency's accounts and tax demands are correct in themselves. Any authorized grants are to be paid to His Excellency according to the payee's wealth until the date scheduled for the grant to run out. However, there were fervent pleas to His Excellency that the exhausted subjects of Lippe should be given a respite, or at least a lower rate of assessment.

2   As regards the upkeep of His Excellency's adjutant, Count Otto of Lippe-Brake [uncle to the young rulers] has reached a separate accommodation agreeing to pay only for the cavalry troop protecting the adjutant, and nothing else. He will do this with the proviso that his part of the tax granted by the Lippe nobility, which is still to be paid in full, be remitted. The Detmold regency councillors could not agree to this and have referred the matter back to the count of Waldeck [the official regent], and they have not accepted it. The towns of Lippe have also offered to

contribute their share for the upkeep of the adjutant's cavalry, without
further prejudice to the original tax agreement.

3   Those route marches of the Emperor's regiments through Lippe
which could not be prevented are also to be paid for in due part by Count
Otto and the towns of Lippe in such a way that the government is
reimbursed for what it paid out in provisions and money, with the
exception of any damage that may have occurred.

4   The costs of delivering war contributions will also be borne by the
towns but only in moderate and due part and not in excess.

5   The towns are to be exempted from the costs of route marches
whenever one or more companies of soldiers hold a night camp, yet with
half or whole regiments they are to negotiate and pay their share. These
regiments are to be provisioned in common and *pro rata* after full
notification has been made [*in gemain auff nachrichtliche anzeige pro rata
vnderhalten*].

6   The towns refuse to contribute to local defence at government level
[*Landrettung*] since they have to make their own urban defence
arrangements, and this item was not agreed at the territorial assembly
[*Landtag*]. Yet the towns do agree to join the home guard [*Landfolge*], and
to support whatever grants towards it may be made at a subsequent
territorial assembly. Against this the Detmold government has openly
taken exception.

7   The costs of distraint for unpaid taxes are to be apportioned
according to the amount owed in arrears.

8   Travel costs, common expenses and payment of messengers are all
referred to further discussion for payment, after which the account will be
closed, finalized and signed by all sides.

9   Payment of rents and pensions is referred for further information and
discussion, especially to inquire into what the original capital was used
for.

10   The restitution of irregularly used monies is a matter for justice and
legal decision in order that no one shall be unfairly treated.

11   Concerning payment of officials' salaries the towns agree to accept
the previously notified accounts of Gevekott [Lemgo patrician and
government official], but they reserve the rest for further discussion.

12   Since for several reasons Count Otto still disagrees with the quotas
that the towns of Lippe have offered to contribute, although they have
been accepted and already called upon for payment by the Detmold
government, so this matter has been postponed until it has been
examined further.

    The [government on behalf of the] young rulers have resolved to apportion the burden fairly throughout the land and ordered that their subjects be granted relief of one sixth on that which they usually pay [in rents], in order that they shall all the more readily pay their assessment, however high that may be, to redeem Lippstadt.

> Signed by Tilly's commissar-general and all the other interested parties.

Minutes taken by von Lerchen, army secretary [*Feldschreiber*].

> Countersigned by Count Otto of Lippe [*Erbherr* from a junior branch of the ruling family],
> *Landdrost* Johann von der Borch [senior local official and head of the nobility],
> Dr Heinrich Kirckman [lawyer for Lemgo town],
> Georg Ziegler [Horn town],
> Antonius Weber [Blomberg town].

> Staatsarchiv Detmold, L 37, XVII 9a

15 The 'salva guardia' fails in Anhalt, 1636

A letter of protection (*salva guardia*) from the Swedish high command is violated by troops under Swedish command. This is an eye-witness account from local official in charge.

Local Scribe [*Amtsschreiber*] Martin Gerlach to Local Councillor[*Amtsrat*] Wiess, from Nienburg, 14 January 1636.

Honourable Sir (etc.)

Immediately after their withdrawal, on both sides of the Saale River we were surrounded by Swedish troops who went up to Bernburg and straight away hacked open the gates, forcibly took away all the horses from the ruling prince's residence and from the burghers here, also plundering various houses. They did the same at Wedlitz whose local official [*Amtmann*], Herr Signitz, they deprived of his personal belongings, also taking both his horses.

When before the plundering, in front of the ruling prince's residence I tried to show them, and request that they respect Swedish Chancellor Oxenstierna's letter of protection [*salva guardia*], I was threatened to be shot and hustled away, my boots were pulled off my feet and what I had collected in fear and haste and had about my person was taken from me with great violence. To date the local official [*Amtmann*] dare not come in here. Now that the damage has been done, four cavalrymen from Mulk's regiment have been sent in to guarantee protection. They are demanding 24 talers. God knows if we are really going to get protection from them.

> Schulz II, 88

16–17   The manufacture of arms in Cologne and Ulm

16   Cologne

During these thirty years the city of Cologne was frequently ordered to supply considerable quantities of armaments to the belligerents because of its high capacity for manufacture and trade. It was usually paid for its deliveries. A few weeks after the revolt of the Bohemians against the Habsburgs in 1618, Cologne received orders for weapons from France and Lorraine. Even if the orders of the Imperialists were later to take up most of the city's capacity, there was still enough to supply the Swedes, from which the city finally managed to free itself in 1632 by diplomatically imposing a general embargo on all exports of weapons and munitions.

The records show that from 1619 the city itself bought much of the war material that it produced. In 1632, for example, the city council placed an order for 3,000 muskets. Yet the once famous manufacture of hand-guns in Cologne had decayed to such an extent in the decades before the Thirty Years War, that its arms dealers often placed commissions with ironworks of surrounding territories, including those in the duchy of Berg, the convent of Essen and the district around Aachen. Cologne gunsmiths had to farm out certain stages of manufacture such as the drilling and smoothing of barrels, which needed machines driven by water power in the duchy of Berg.

The arms purchases of Imperial troops, and of some Rhenish and south German troops, as well as of the Dutch were substantial. In the accounts for 1634 the Imperial army ordered

  1,000 breast-plates at 8 reichstalers each,
  2,000 smaller pieces of armour at $3\frac{1}{2}$ rtlr,
  1,000 pairs of pistols at $7\frac{1}{2}$ rtlr,
  3,000 carbines at $3\frac{1}{2}$ rtlr,
  2,000 muskets at $2\frac{1}{2}$ rtlr,
  1,500 whole and 500 half pikes at $\frac{1}{2}$ rtlr each.

The city council acted as surety for the manufacturers and paid them with promissory notes which were traded as legal tender. In 1636 the Imperialists ordered another 4,000 breast-plates, and in 1642 even the city of Aachen had canon cast in Cologne. Year after year contracts for arms went to Cologne where they were often subcontracted by its factors to the surrounding countryside, above all to the duchy of Berg for blades, or to the county of Mark for smaller components such as buckles. During the war Cologne merchants also traded Solingen blades to west Europe.

In a similar manner Aachen and its surrounding districts supplied arms
and uniforms to the Imperial armies.

> B. Kuske, *Köln, der Rhein und das Reich*
> (Cologne, 1956), 190–91

17 Ulm

In 1646 the Ulm district chronicler, Heberle, wrote:

Every day several hundred Swedes went shopping in the city of Ulm, and I
saw this with my own eyes, for we have once again unwillingly had [to flee
from our village] to find living accommodation in the city. Since there are
more Swedes than Imperial troops camped outside Ulm, the city fathers
have organized the manufacture of overcoats and many pairs of shoes.
They have given the money back to the Swedish army and also supplied
them with many horses.

Heberle's editor comments:

Ulm's deliveries of coats, shoes and horses to the Swedes were significant.
A coat was valued at 9 fl and a horse at 60 fl. The demand made by the
French under Turenne ran to 4,000 coats, 1,000 pairs of shoes and 300
horses. Ulm city council desperately tried to reduce this almost
impossibly high demand, and in a letter of 14 September offered exactly
one half of the amount. Agreement was then reached for the supply of
1,000 grey woollen coats, 1,000 pairs of shoes, 58 horses equipped with
saddles, reins and pistols, and 40 hundredweight of gunpowder.

> Heberle, 209–10

18–20 Shipping

18 Dutch prize money for Spanish shipping, 1632

The States General have proffered great reward to all those that will
attempt any thing against the enemy by sea.

Those that shall bring in any prize of the enemies ships, barques, boats,
ponts, shaloupes, etc. shall be thus requited: he that takes a ship

of above an hundred last	30,000 gilders
of above 70 to an hundred	20,000
50 to 70	15,000
30 to 50	10,000
20 to 30	8,000

for a pinnace under 20 last,
provided with four murderers 4,000 gilders
   for a boat with 12 oars on a side 8,000 gilders
   for a shaloup of 8 oars   2,000
               6 oars   1,200
               4 oars   600

If in case the ship, pinnace, boat or shaloup shall chance to be strand
or miscarry, those that take the same, shall then only receive the one half
of the promised reward.

Forraine Avisoes (London), no. 18 (April 14
1632), 10

19–20 Hamburg and Dover shipping compared

19 Entry and exit of ships paying admiralty-toll at Hamburg, 1646

	Entry	Exit
From the German Baltic ports	38	18
Other Baltic lands	4	2
Norway	14	12
Sweden	18	12
England	16	28
(Dover	nil	10)
Scotland	2	nil
Shetlands	9	9
France	41	27
Italy	5	4
Spanish Netherlands	4	nil
Russia	2	4
Spain and Portugal	41	51
West Indies	5	5

M. Reissmann, *Die Hamburgische Kaufmannschaft des 17. Jahrhunderts* (Hamburg, 1975),
370–71

20 Numbers of ships carrying re-exports from Dover, 1638

		Of the foreign ships:	
Dover	144	French	11
London	60	Flemish	13
In the Downs, specified by		German	48
master's name only	39	(Hamburg	31)

Other English	71	Dutch	5
Foreign	94	Norway	4
		Other	13

J. S. Kepler, *The Exchange of Christendom: the International Entrepôt at Dover, 1622–51* (Leicester, 1976), 162–4

21 Plunder and the blackmarket

The Battle of Nördlingen is described in a village cobbler's diary within the context of his own existence. He is plundered by his own side and by the enemy, and much later mentions a decree against the blackmarket in stolen goods which was unenforceable.

[1634] After capturing Regensburg the king of Hungary [the future Emperor Ferdinand III] travelled up the Danube with his armies. When Duke Bernhard [of Saxe-Weimar] and Colonel Horn [for the Swedes] realized this, they set about burning and laying waste Bavaria, arriving at the Danube near Laungingen. Since they were in great haste to occupy Württemberg before the Imperial troops reached it, Duke Bernhard immediately crossed the Danube. His army had been ruined in Bavaria, and since his riders had nearly all lost their horses, he arrived in our territory of Ulm with his whole army.

Since we did not regard him as an enemy, and since we had not been warned by our authorities to regard his army as such, we had hidden nothing, keeping horses, cattle and all our meagre household possessions openly about us. But Duke Bernhard's troops broke into our land and plundered us completely of horses, cattle, bread, flour, salt, lard, cloth, linen, clothes and everything we possessed. They maltreated the people, shooting, stabbing and beating a number of people to death. No settlement was strong enough to resist, although several tried it but they fared even worse as a result of the attempt. We tried to resist here in our village of Weidenstetten [about four hours by horseback to the north of Ulm city], but we failed, although we held out bravely for two days, driving off several fierce bands of riders, by keeping all our cattle and horses in the churchyard and all our belongings in the church. But while we were holding out at the church, they set alight the village and burnt down five houses and five stables.

Once that had happened, each one of us went to look after his own property, and common defence collapsed. Several hundred riders appeared, plundering and taking everything they could drag or carry with them. Cattle and horses all went, at least those of them they could catch,

and very few beasts were left behind. This happened at Weidenstetten on
10 August. [Ulm territory claimed the loss of 2,000 horses to Duke
Bernhard's troops on this day alone].

On 22 August my fifth child was born to my dear wife between one and
two in the afternoon. He was given the name of Bartholomew and
christened on the same day, a Friday.

After we had survived this theft and plunder, and since it was just
harvest time, we went and cut our corn and carried it home as best we
could since we had few horses left. The summer crop was not ready but
unripe.

Duke Bernhard's horsemen and footsoldiers moved into the Riess
district around Bopfingen and Neresheim, where they struck camp and
were joined by the Württemberg levies [*ausschuss*], and the Rhine count is
also expected to bring his troops to join Duke Bernhard. In the meantime
the Imperial army reached Nördlingen and besieged it. Both sides faced
each other for a fortnight. The Imperialists tried to attack and storm
Nördlingen several times but failed. Duke Bernhard tried to help the
defenders but little did he realize in what strength the Imperialists had
appeared. And so he went with three hundred riders and cut through the
enemy straight into the town of Nördlingen, which now became Swedish.
[In fact it was not Duke Bernhard but Gustav Horn who undertook this
defence.] They defended themselves so bravely that the enemy could
achieve nothing.

But after both sides had skirmished nearly every day, Duke Bernhard
and Gustav Horn marched their armies out and bravely attacked the
enemy on 27 August. Their numbers were too small since the Rhine count
had not arrived with his troops. The Imperialists were very powerful and
outnumbered the Swedes two to one. At first the Imperialists were beaten
and driven back, yet this did not last and the Swedes were thoroughly
defeated. Since all was lost, Gustav Horn captured and Duke Bernhard
wounded, his army was ruined and it fled. Fugitive riders reached us
already by midday. When we understood what had happened, we wasted
no time and anyone who could run took to his legs in order to reach Ulm
city on that same day. We appreciated the fact that the enemy was now
after us, and the Swedes were no better. What they could steal they took
with them as they fled, and so we had both sides on our neck.

We had to leave all our belongings behind. We were fortunate to escape
with wife and child, and just had to leave the rest. As soon as the battle was
lost, the king of Hungary attacked the town of Nördlingen, which
surrendered for lack of further aid. The town council and burghers
begged him for mercy, which was granted. Nördlingen then became the

first Protestant Union town after Regensburg to fall into the hands of the king of Hungary.

After this the king of Hungary moved into Württemberg with his army. There was a great scare in Ulm, since it was feared that he was also after the city. Together with the citizens we were ordered to clear the beautiful wood in front of the Gate of Our Lady and everything was brought into the city.

Because the troops were in pursuit of their enemies, they laid waste to everything, plundered the beautiful little town of Giengen and burnt it down. The town of Geisslingen in Ulm territory weakly tried to defend itself. It was overrun and several hundred people were massacred. The pastor had his head cut off, and the place was devastated. The duchy of Württemberg shared a similar fate.

In sum, I can not exaggerate the dreadful events from those times. They went straight through our territory and their night camp was held between Neenstetten and Weidenstetten on the Blumenberg [villages where the author lived to the north of Ulm city]. Our hamlets were badly damaged and the king of Hungary himself stayed the night in Weidenstetten.

On 17 September we returned home [to Weidenstetten village from Ulm city] to harvest what the riders had left of our summer crops and also to sow a few fields with new corn. On 19 September my son Bartholomew died between seven and eight in the morning, aged four weeks. May Almighty God give him a joyful resurrection on the last day of judgement, and grant him eternal life.

On 4 October many Imperial troops arrived at Günzburg and Leipheim, plundering the surrounding countryside. Everyone had to flee to the city [of Ulm] once more, and we stayed the whole winter there. There was real hardship, famine and dearth. We were crowded together and lived in great want. Hunger and price increase came at the same time, and after that the evil disease, the pest. Many hundred people died of it in this year and also in the next.

On 7 October while we were in flight my son Thomas died at Jungingen between eleven and twelve at night, and he was buried there the next morning. May Almighty God give him a joyful resurrection on the last day of judgement and grant him eternal life. This is the third time we had to flee from home.

On 30 November my stepmother died between five and six in the evening. On 1 December between four and five in the morning my sister Barbara died and on the next day my sister Dorothea died between six and seven in the morning. On 18 December my sister Ursel died between

eleven and twelve at midday. May Almighty God give them all a joyful
resurrection on the last day of judgement and grant them eternal life. On
29 December I returned home to Weidenstetten where we survived the
winter.

In this year corn was very expensive and the Ulm imen was 9 to 12
gulden, rye was up to 8 gulden, lard 7 batzen [almost one half gulden] per
pound, and salt cost 10 batzen per metzen. A calf cost 12 to 15 gulden in
the city. . . .

[1646] Since so much had been stolen by the troops, taken into Ulm city
by army suppliers and soldiers, and purchased by citizens and peasants,
the clergy preached earnestly against the practice and condemned it from
the pulpit. It was also banned by the authorities several times, but that
helped very little and it did not stop, instead everything could be bought
that way. And since army suppliers bought up and carried away all the
corn and bread they could find, hoarding took place, driving prices to 5
gulden, when the whole previous year corn prices had hardly risen above
3 gulden per imen, and rye had been as low as 20 batzen and at most 24
batzen.

Heberle, 148–53, 212–13

22   The Sack of Magdeburg, 1631

This official Swedish report of the Sack of Magdeburg by the Catholic League
blames the citizenry. A letter from Salvius to the Riksråd, Hamburg, May 1631.

It is quite certain now that Magdeburg was stormed at the first attempt on
10 May [1631], and the whole big city is lying in ashes. For as long as
possible Marshal Falkenberg tried to keep the enemy out of the outer
defences. The enemy made several attempts to take the smaller defences
and lost many people before finally succeeding. Yet since there were less
than 2,000 defenders against 24,000 besiegers, no people were spared by
the enemy to attack the city day and night without respite. The defenders
were given no relief and had to lie on the defences day and night, keeping
awake and repulsing wave after wave of attackers. . . . The enemy was
able to fill the moat by ordering peasants from the whole surrounding
countryside to bring brushwood which was then cast into the moat for it
had mostly dried up. The enemy then entrenched themselves in the
defences and when the general storm was ordered, riders passed through
the breach across the moat and through the defences. The footsoldiers
soon attacked the other fast places within the city. Whoever they
encountered, they slew. They raped wives and virgins, tyrannized young
and old . . . and spared no one.

The whole city was plundered until it was bare. Finally, everything was set alight and totally burnt down. Only the cathedral and four or five adjoining houses and a few fishermen's cottages along the River Elbe survived.

I spoke to a cavalryman who was in the city throughout the siege, and who was saved by a corporal in the enemy army who happened to be a friend. The day after the enemy first stormed the city he went through the streets, and reports that Falkenberg was offered terms, but that he and his soldiers refused them, since the main demand was that all soldiers and citizens should become Catholic and surrender unconditionally to the Imperialists. Falkenberg's corpse was lying plundered and naked in the market square. It was then dragged into a burning house where the flames consumed it as the house fell in. The Protestant administrator of Magdeburg received a light gunshot in his side and a sword blow over the head. He has been taken prisoner and is now in Tilly's camp. . . .

About three hundred citizens were on the side of the Emperor. When the enemy first broke into the city, they ran to greet them but were the first to be slaughtered. A large section of the citizenry fled into the cathedral and bolted the doors so effectively that no one could get to them on the first day of pillage. On the following day terms of surrender were announced and they were pardoned. But those who hoped to save themselves by fleeing to the other churches were all massacred. The clergy were most terribly treated. They were first massacred in their library and then burnt along with their books. Their wives and daughters were tied behind the horses, dragged into camp, raped and terribly molested.

The church of St John was full of womenfolk, whom they locked in from the outside, thereafter throwing burning torches through the windows. The Croats and Walloons behaved mercilessly, throwing children into the fire and tying the more beautiful and well-off women citizens to their stirrups, made off with them behind their horses out of town. They spiked small children onto their lances, waved them around and cast them into the flames. Turks, Tartars and heathens could not have been more cruel.

A number of malcontents blame His Majesty [Gustavus Adolphus], who had promised them aid, for failing to rescue them. That help was so long in being prepared is not His Majesty's fault. The city could well have held out longer, if the citizenry had offered the defending garrison more assistance and been somewhat less self-confident. To start with they allowed no defending soldiers into the city, and instead these soldiers had to remain in the suburbs and live on money actually supplied by His Majesty. Finally, they were let into the city where the cellars and stores

were well filled, yet the defending soldiers had to suffer hunger or buy
every morsel of food in cash at very high prices. In this way they were very
weakened. Everywhere there were secret contacts with the enemy, who
started by offering terms to the city. But while these were being considered
and while the citizens considered themselves quite securely defended, the
enemy stormed the place and so made a mockery of their complacency.

Schulz I, 95–6

23   The plague

Reports of epidemics from Prague (1638) and Vienna (1643) illustrate one of the
commonplaces of seventeenth-century life.

In the royal capital of Prague the infectious epidemic of pestilence and
other poisonous weaknesses have started to rage mightily, to the extent
that as well as the ecclesiastics, so also other secular persons have fled in
great number out of the town into the surrounding villages where a not
inconsiderable misery was to be observed.

For even on the fields and other properties hideous worms were
perceived, which were contained in the seeds and roots of the cereals,
which ate out kernel and essence, causing great damage. . . .

Seeing that the plague seemed also likely to break out in St Pölten, the
Emperor himself escaped from there towards Melk on 24 August, and as
he could not feel more secure in that place he moved further up [the
Danube] towards Linz on the first day of autumn.

For the same plague raged at Vienna and in this whole region along
with red dysentery, doing considerable damage to the Imperial
army. Among others the archduke's senior court chamberlain, Count
Harrach, was brought ill to Vienna where he died some hours after his
arrival.

The Swedes have also not been free from this dysentery which seems to
have occurred because of overeating fruit, especially plums and grapes.
Also those regiments which were under General Douglas with the
Transylvanians have from this contact brought the plague back,
wherefore they have to camp separately.

H. Jessen (ed.), *Der dreissigjährige Krieg* (second
edition, Düsseldorf, 1964), 377–8, 392

24   The effects of war

A Protestant clergyman, Superintendent Andreä, looks back at the effects of war
on the town of Calw in Württemberg. From a letter to a friend.

Through murder, plunder, beating and burning, taking of people and other destructive activities, we have been reduced to one third of our population. We were 3,832 and we have lost 2,304, leaving only 1,528 of us. Those of us who remain would consider ourselves fortunate if only, as is granted to various other destroyed places, we were left alone to assess our own losses which are in excess of a ton of gold, but instead we are further burdened so that our ruinous condition will finally exhaust and flatten us. The number of destitute is so large that they run to 500 or 600 head and in our town treasury there is not one farthing left. From among the citizens alone there are 125 persons in the hospital and even more still in their houses who have to be supplied regularly. It is not possible to say how much this relief costs us, since even the richest can hardly supply their own families with necessities.

Yet we would perhaps have been able to bear these costs since Christian love always finds a way with charity, if only the fierce war tax paid to ward off plundering [*Brandschatzung*] for a third time had not sucked us dry. Our poor town had to pay 800 gulden *per week* over and above the fixed rate. It was collected with extreme severity and it came on top of all our existing worries, especially since plague and hunger claim 100 to 150 victims monthly from among our ranks, so that those who remain alive also have to pay the tax assessments of the dead.

However, this was not the sum total of our plight. You know that all our livelihood consisted of weaving and dyeing of cloth, and if we lost or were prevented from carrying out these activities, then a knife would really be at our throats, since we depend on this work. With all the destruction and shrinkage of population we still have 243 master craftsmen in this profession. Yet they have no employment, to their great vexation. Added to them are another 64 from the immediate neighbourhood, who, like us, are out of work. But the gloom still does not end there. As the fable says, when the stomach is denied nourishment, all the members suffer, so one can say about Calw that when this [textile manufacture] is blocked, the whole neighbourhood must bleed to death. In the vicinity there are 1,200 textile workers who depend on the town for contracts, as well as a similar amount or even more women spinners, as I know for certain from the registers. When Calw starves, most of the region around it starves too. . . .

That is why our town also should be subsidised or given tax-relief for reason of state [*aus Staatsraison*], which those who go around in arms thinking only of their own immediate advantage just can not grasp or heed. There should be an end to all this now, especially after the destruction and immoderate levies of war tax that we have had to pay for a frightful half year now, during which time 800 of us have died, whose burial has cost us at least 100 gulden. The cost of caring for the sick in upkeep and medicines runs to more than 1,000 gulden. . . .

I am not so hard-bitten that I do not also remember with horror the destruction of so many honourable married women, so many men and woman citizens of whom on one day alone we buried 83, and about whom we will keep a record. One should also include violated women and virgins, and the young men, the flower of the town who were led away to certain ruin in body and soul.

I can well appreciate that our fate can not compare with that of Magdeburg, Bautzen and other famous cities. Yet, since each one has a sore wound and since in a large city each house has its own cross, so it can surely be allowed for me to lament my own place and people. All the more so since over many years I have got to know my flock very well and they are second to none in praising God, in obedience to the authorities and willingness to help, thrifty in housekeeping and generous to the needy. I could not be expected to tell this without being affected by it, although it is usually the duty of the historian to be objective. . . .

What I demand is for the good of my congregation and I am prepared after the loss of a serious part of my property to be stoical and see beyond things that are material. For my own part, however, I could not claim that I am experiencing serious poverty. I still have a number of comforts and can not praise highly enough the readiness of others to be kind to me. Those who really are destitute and nearly dying are worst off, especially since the diminishing wealth of a number of substantial families is no longer sufficient for the upkeep of so many ruined families. Former rich and landed people whose houses once were like open hospitals and harbours to refugees now live in squalor and extreme parsimony, from which you can easily gather what a dreadful fate the poor people are suffering.

Yet the war-tax collectors are threatening us anew with beatings and burnings, with torture and forced labour. If they are allowed to carry on like this we will all soon be dead and in such a way we would escape their violence, if only my dread of what would then happen to all the remaining orphans who would suffer all manner of injustice did not sorely trouble my heart.

You would hardly believe the fact that among those who have starved and frozen to death there were people who once had over 1,000 gulden a year in income. I saw the orphans of a former merchant who had an inheritance of 15,000 gulden wandering aimlessly through the streets. They were finally only taken into the homes of their relatives by command

of the authorities. You can hardly imagine the liberties that are taken with
the poor as they lie dying in their own filth. Corpses are often found in
front of the gravedigger's home, their shrouds and linen plundered, lying
quite naked there, since even rags are at a premium. It is not worth
speaking of medicines or palliatives since there are no doctors, chemists
or barbers left, in whose place only the hangman or extortioner remains.

Still, the few of us who remain alive do so more as a miracle of God than
by nature, art or at the help of any human kind. We live and celebrate our
church services freely. Sins, which occur all the more readily in these
anarchic times and which go unpunished more than is usually the case, we
publicly castigate. We give new heart to those who are defeatist and
depressed, and as far as we are able, we give real aid to those who have
suffered misfortune. After all, why should we complain when from all
sides we only hear complaints in reply, which, however, often turn out to
be laughable since the smallest of craftsmen sometimes makes a great
noise over ten gulden worth of damage, whereas we have to keep silent
when we lose 100 or 1,000 gulden, although we have no place to turn for
support?

> Johann Valentin Andreä: *Ein Schwäbischer
> Pfarrer im Dreissigjährigen Krieg*, edited by P.
> Antony and H. Christmann (Heidenheim,
> 1970), 90–94

25   War damage, 1645

We then put horses, cattle and all our belongings into the church. We
cleared all our barns, collected all the corn from the fields and threshed it.
Then we took it away together with wife and child. That was our best
defence, until we lost everything.

On 23 September the French and the Bavarian armies broke camp and
both went up the Neckar through Württemberg as far as Tübingen and
the Black Forest. And if thieves had not succeeded in robbing us of our
corn we would have been able to survive very well during our next exile in
Ulm city. But we fared badly.

On 25 September, just after we were robbed, the whole district fled
once again to Ulm city. On the same night I fell ill and lay sick in Ulm for
four weeks with wife and child, using up all the savings that I had rescued
from the robbers. This was the twenty-second time we villagers have had
to seek refuge in the city.

On 17 October my little daughter Dorothea died between eight and
nine in the morning in Ulm where we had sought refuge, and she was

GERMANY IN THE THIRTY YEARS WAR

buried there. May God give her a joyful resurrection on the last day of judgement, and grant her eternal life.

On 21 December on St Thomas's Day a company of Lapier's Bavarian cavalry were billeted on us, and they were on the Imperial side. On 24 and 25 December they moved towards the Upper Palatinate where Swedish troops were marauding.

This was a harsh war year with much plundering, thieving and crime, as well as causing extra expenses and war tax payments. The Imperial Sallisch regiment which was lodged during the summer in the local district [*Amt*] of Albeck alone cost the following amounts:

Langenau had to provide and pay in money	4,558 fl 36 kr
Albeck *Amt*	4,431 fl 30 kr
Altheim *Amt*	1,391 fl
Balendorf *Amt*	1,266 fl
Weidenstetten *Amt*	2,152 fl 30 kr
Bernstater *Amt*	1,582 fl 30 kr
Edelschiesser *Amt*	316 fl 30 kr

Total 15,740 gulden 36 Kreuzer

God be praised, it was a time of good harvest and fair prices for the imen of corn was usually below 2 gulden with rye at 1 taler and all cereals in plentiful supply. And God pleases Himself in order that poor and rich shall pray and call upon his bounty.

Heberle, 204–5

26 Relative prosperity
Pastor Dietwar's wine sales, 1617–29 (see above, p. xvi, for a note on coinage and measures).

Proceeds from the sale of wine from my vineyard at Hoheim village in Franconia, 1617–29.

1617 For 18 eimer of new wine at 20 fl per fuder, comes to	30 fl	
1618 For 15 eimer less 16 mass (and one gulden to the wife)	32 fl	
1619 For 19 eimer of new wine	54 fl	
and for 10½ eimer of perry (and to the wife one rhenish gulden for purchases)	36 fl	
1620 For 17½ eimer	45 fl	
For 8 eimer less 7 mass of the 1619 vintage	26 fl	11 batzen

1621 For 14½ eimer at 74 fl to the fuder (and to the wife 7 ort for purchases)	90 fl	
1622 In March for 18 eimer, 19 mass at 1 ducat to the eimer, and the ducat at 16 fl (and to the wife one taler for purchases)		
On 22 September for 19 eimer, 26 mass of the 1621 vintage at 39 rtlr to the fuder, and ½ taler for purchases	74 fl	6 batzen
1623 On 7 July for 19½ eimer at 6 fl to the eimer of 1622 vintage	117 fl	
1624 On 1 March for 1 fuder and 1 mass of 1623 vintage	63 fl	
On 10 August for 18 eimer, 19 mass at 4½ fl to the eimer of 1623 vintage	82 fl	
1625 On 3 February for 6 eimer at 4 fl 1½ ort to the eimer of 1623 vintage	26 fl	¼ batzen
For 21 eimer 1624 vintage	70 fl	
1626 On 15 January for 19 eimer and 14 mass of 1624 vintage received from the keeper of the Star Inn at Nuremberg, and 1 tlr for purchases, in all	109 fl	
On 13 May for 10½ eimer of 1625 vintage at 48 fl to the fuder	41 fl	13 batzen
On 23 September for 8 eimer of 1625 vintage at 70 fl to the fuder, and ½ taler for purchases	52 fl	10 batzen
1627 On 2 July for 11½ eimer of 1625 vintage at 77 fl to the fuder	73 fl	½ tlr
1628 Nothing		
1629 On 6 February for 22 eimer, 14 mass of 1627 vintage	144 fl	

And the total of all these sales of wine that I made came to 1,132 gulden. May God be praised and thanked for this. The total of wine sold came to 24 fuder [48,000 litres]. So God's little fountain in Hoheim did not just splash water but also wine in abundance. To Him be praised.

Pastor Dietwar's salary at Kitzingen under the Swedes, 1633–5.

Account of annual pay earned by the three former deacons at Kitzingen and the arrears in pay that are still owed to them.

From Kitzingen monastery the deacons earned yearly because of the monastery parish.

In money   34 fl
    Item: 10 fl 7 pounds and 22 pennies in penny tithe
In corn   4 malter and 3 malter wheat
In wine   14 eimer
    Item: 3 eimer wine tithe
In wood   ½ morgen

From holding, as was done earlier, a sermon on all Sundays and holidays in this place and receiving pay in lieu of a meal for it 25 fl 4 pounds and 6 pence.

The pay granted up to now by His Majesty the King of Sweden to the four colleges, monasteries and parish pastors and the two deacons, as shared,

In money   100 fl
In corn   9 malter and 1 malter wheat [1,200 kilos]
In wine   1 fuder.

From the hospital for its chaplaincy and for the monastery parish,

In money   24 fl
In corn   9 malter
In wine   14 eimer
In wood   4 fuder [or four-horse-drawn cartloads].

Owed by the commoners of the town   300 fl
Owed from the Reumann-Weyerisch foundation   15 fl

These salaries were fully paid during the government of the Swedish king as regards the items from the monastery and the hospital, but salary from the common town and from the Reumann-Weyerisch foundation was never paid.

Furthermore, in the period when the town of Kitzingen was under the government of the margraves of Brandenburg from 30 September 1633 until our displacement on 19 March 1635 [by the Catholics from Würzburg], in other words for a full 1½ years. . . . [There follow heavy arrears as the Brandenburg Franconian government fell heavily behind with payments.]

(Bartholomäus Dietwar, *Leben eines evangelischen Pfarrers im früheren markgräflichen Amte Kitzingen von 1592–1670 von ihm selbst erzählt*, edited by V. Wirth (Kitzingen, 1887), 60–61, 98–100

III Religion and propaganda

An outbreak of hostilities was likely to provide grist to the mill of any self-styled prophet of doom, as the diarist, Hans Heberle, who was a master cobbler, part-time peasant and devout Lutheran in a village north of Ulm city, was at pains to point out (43). In his account he followed (at times verbatim) a fly-sheet that he may have acquired and read in Ulm, the city to which he fled countless times with his family since soldiers and bandits regularly made village existence impossible for brief periods of time (compare 40). Yet the final string-puller was the Almighty and, at least in traditional Lutheran fashion, His mind was inscrutable. It was best, therefore, not to swear, sin or tempt God (29, 31) but once having done so, the sermon, moralizing pamphlet and prayer session were available to propitiate Him and give mere mortals a blanket explanation. People were extraordinarily inventive in apportioning blame (or praise – see 28) after the event (27, 30), and even somewhat smug in thanking the Lord for having preserved them from worse excesses suffered by their fellow humans (39).

Journalism played an increasingly large part in these war years and it enmeshed superstition, religion and practical politics, even giving vent to secular and national feelings. The latter, however, may best be left to the preoccupations of nineteenth-century historians who, perhaps inevitably, ransacked seventeenth-century chronicles, fly-sheets and news-books for this kind of interpretation (36). The unrealistic 'adventure story' of war, seen at a safe distance, was then an 'entertainment' just as much as it seems to be today. Yet examples of the range and sophistication of journalism come from the London of King Charles I. Document (34) is sheer stop-gap entertainment to hide the lack of real news. Document (35) is a well chosen, accurate piece of seventeenth-century translation concerning official news of importance to understanding the further conduct of the war in Germany. The final months of Gustavus Adolphus's career also show how religion, diplomacy and war were officially quite inseparable (27, 32, 33). Although these examples are Protestant, the Catholics used similar techniques to show that God was on their side (**28**), as is further shown in the career of Ferdinand II (**68–9**).

27   The start of the war, 1617

The war seen as the Catholics' reaction to the Protestants' celebration of the Luther centenary, 1617.

In the year 1617 a Lutheran celebration was held of Dr Martin Luther, the highly esteemed and valued prophet of Germany, the shining light that brought forth again the word of God. To commemorate this all Lutheran churches held a feast of joy and all the children in the territory of Ulm were given a special half batzen coin [worth 2 kreuzer] to mark the occasion. Especial sermons and prayers were composed and held in the churches, some of which I have noted but can not retell here since they are so long, yet they were much written about. The celebration was held on St Martin's Day, 11 November 1617. It was the start of the war as one can read in all the Catholic accounts since this celebration was to them a very sore wound.

Heberle, 92–3

28   The Battle of the White Mountain, 1620

According to this account from Maximilian of Bavaria (retold when the question of this cleric's canonization was being considered), the generals of the Catholic League and of the Austrian Emperor risked the Battle of the White Mountain which they so decisively won only after a fiery speech from a certain Father Dominicus.

When the armies of the League and the Empire had united for the purpose of attacking, with all possible force, the enemy, and the latter had arrived before the walls of Prague, some of the highest officers were averse to the hazard of battle. . . .

When the father observed this, he came up and humbly and modestly requested that it might be permitted him to say a few words, although he had not been called to the council.

When permission was given him, he exhorted the leaders with a fiery zeal that they put their trust in God and the righteousness of their cause; they should firmly trust that the grace of God would not be withheld, and that their hopes would be rewarded with victory. These words moved those who opposed the battle to yield, and with united forces to close upon the foe.

A. Gindely, History of the Thirty Years War I
(London, 1885), vii–ix

29   A decree against swearing, 1638

On 17 August [1638] the worthy city council in Ulm issued and posted another decree against heavy swearing, ordering that any culprits be very strictly punished. [And from another account] on 17 August 1638 a decree against swearing was passed by Ulm city council, and straight away someone was fined 4 gulden and put into the stocks for all to see.

Heberle, 174 and note 299

30   Divine intervention, 1647

The cured pork turns rotten, Wiedenbrück, Westphalia, 1647.

In this month [January] all over Westphalia much of the cured pork went bad, which surprised everyone. And people buried it in the ground. Some say it was because of the warm winter weather but others think that it is an especial punishment from God, and soon the same diseases will fall on the inhabitants just like this mishap occurred with the cured pork. May the Lord God turn away all misfortune.

The editor notes that as in every emergency salt was scarce and probably hoarded. A cold winter may have preserved the inadequately prepared meat. Ascribing the mishap to God closed further inquiry and instilled obedience to religion through superstition and fear.

Andreas Kothe, *Chronik*, edited by F. Flaskamp (Gütersloh, 1962), 21, 61

31   The Catholic takeover in Lutheran Kitzingen, 1629

Great rumbling was often heard in the church at this time. The newly built wall at the Valter tower suddenly collapsed of its own accord one night. Lightning struck the Valter tower and knocked the bells out. Master Claus N., who was a stonemason and master craftsman in the town, also said that he had experienced the following. When he was temporarily living in the house which belonged to Kaspar Neubert opposite the church gable above the parish church, in his sleep during the middle of the night he once felt that the gable of the parish church was collapsing. He got out of bed and looked out of the window to make certain, and only then did he notice that the gable was still standing. But he had another feeling that the coat of arms of the [Protestant] margraves of Brandenburg was still visible. Then two men in long black cloaks came and knocked down the margraves' coat of arms and put the [Catholic] Würzburg arms in its place. Then it seemed that a man came in the air from the direction of Schweinfurt *leading a lion*, and he gave the Würzburg arms a kick so that they clattered down to the churchyard below. The man now replaced the margraves' coat of arms. The vision then disappeared. Master Claus told this to a number of close friends at the time it happened, and before the bishop of Würzburg had taken the town over fully. But after the town of Kitzingen had been taken from the bishop again by the king of Sweden, the dean asked him in the presence of us other pastors as we were just leaving the church whether *the man with the lion* has now arrived and whether he could recognize him [i.e. in the likeness of the king of Sweden]. Master Claus [on seeing the picture] straight away said, 'Yes, that's him.'

On 10 January [1629] the bishop of Würzburg received in person the homage of Kitzingen. Thereafter he went into the church, held mass and demanded the keys to the parish, hospital and Etwashäuser church. After that the first popish sermon was held in the parish church on 11 January.

An omen foretelling the revenge of Gustavus Adolphus.

On 7 September [1631] by the grace of God, the king of Sweden won a noble victory over Tilly and thereafter he occupied Königshofen on 29 September. Once the Swedish army had entered Franconia in full force the popish priests [*Pfaffen*] spent no time in disguising themselves, and with their cooks and housekeepers they ran away. The Swedish soldiers then began to torment the Catholic priests and monks, since they were the cause of the war, and because they had hunted down the Protestants so cruelly.

Dietwar, 49–50, 71–2

32 Gustavus Adolphus's fourteen points to the Emperor

No agreement was reached on these points and no negotiations took place. The talks ended as they were overtaken by the events of war.

When the time came for the appointed negotiations, which was the beginning of April 1630, Freiherr Carl Hannibal von Dona appeared for His Imperial Majesty. On the Swedish side there was a commissar, and there were also the envoys of the king of Denmark. But the negotiations did not progress and in all the three months that von Dona stayed in Danzig nothing was decided until finally the negotiations broke off when news was received of the Swedish army landings on German soil.

The points which the king of Sweden proposed for setting up a negotiated peace were as follows:

1   The Emperor must withdraw all troops from the Upper and Lower Saxon Circles.

2   All defences and forts which have been constructed since the start of this German war at the Baltic and North Sea coast are to be removed.

3   Where the above Circles touch the Baltic and North Sea coast no garrisons whatsoever are to remain.

4   All harbours and ports are to be returned to the condition that they were in before the war, nor are they to be used to equip warships and armadas, and those that are under construction are to be broken up.

5   Concerning the bishoprics of the territorial princes whose lands adjoin the Baltic and North Sea coast, one should follow the rulings of the Electors and Estates of the Empire.

6   In each of the Saxon Circles the following members above all are to be reinstated: the dukes of Pomerania and of Mecklenburg, as well as the counts of Oldenburg and of East Frisia, and the towns especially are to be returned in prewar condition.

7   If it is proved that anyone has transgressed against the Emperor and the Empire, then he is to be punished with a fine, according to the decision of the Electors and Estates of the Empire.

8   In order that the dukes of Mecklenburg may be reinstated swiftly and fully, the king of Sweden offers to act as surety for any fine that they may be condemned to pay, and they are to be reinstated forthwith.

9   The Swedish occupation of Stralsund shall cease, and when the city recovers its former privileges, all costs and damages that it has suffered during the siege are to be made good.

10   Neither now nor in the future is it to be held against the king of Sweden that he gave aid to the city of Stralsund.

11   His Imperial Majesty must promise not to aid the enemies of the king and crown of Sweden.

12   All injuries and misunderstandings are to be forgotten permanently and from now on there shall be genuine peace and friendship between His Imperial Majesty and the king of Sweden.

13   In this peace and in its negotiation the kings of France, Great Britain and Denmark are to be included, as also the Estates General of the United Netherlands.

14   The agreement is to be signed and sealed by all parties who are concerned and who have a major interest in the peace.

P. Arlanibaeus (Abelin), *Arma Svecica* (no place given, 1632), 7–8

33   English praise of Gustavus Adolphus, 1632

In 1632 a news-sheet called *The Swedish Intelligencer* gave Londoners news primarily of the Swedish involvement in the wars in Germany. The sheet was pro-Protestant and called Gustavus Adolphus 'Caesar and Alexander of our times' in its preface. It praised the information given in former *Weekly Currantoes*, and asked for information from any English gentleman of news from abroad to be sent to it – an early plea for 'foreign correspondents'.

We have everywhere dealt candidly, not magnifying the [Swedish] king, nor derogating from his enemies; not left out, or put in, for favour, or advantage. Our method is this: to handle every story by it self, and then to bring all together at the day of battle. Careful have we been to note the times and to describe the places of the most famous actions.

The Imperial Diet of Ratisbon, which was well hoped would have mended all, leaving things far more desperate in the Protestant party, necessitated a resolution in the princes of the Confession; rather to die free, then to live slaves. Hence their Diet of Leipzig.

And because of these Leaguers were at first of an union by themselves, we have briefly first handled their warlike preparations, until the day of their joining with the king.

The same have we done with the king's story: gone along with it from his Majesty's first landing.

Cambridge University Library, Acton.d.sel. 601, 2, 3

34   A children's war-game, 1632

In the early spring of 1632 schoolchildren were encouraged to play a war-game. In this version, from a contemporary newspaper, the Catholics get the worst of it. The story probably circulated also with events and outcome in reverse.

Letter from Ratisbon, 6 March 1632.

Because I have no other news at this time, give me leave to impart unto you a ridiculous but true relation of what happened this last Shrovetide at Chin, a good town as you know in the Upper Palatinate.

The dean, mayor and town clerk there, whether for pastime only or out of desire to make some prognostication, have encouraged the schoolboys, of both the schools that are there to play the soldiers, and make the burgomaster his son to be Tilly, who went about through all the town, with his drums to gather his soldiers, such of the schoolboys, as voluntarily would come and take his party; and gathered of them above one hundred and fifty.

Afterwards it was desired to have also a king of Sweden, but then being found none that durst accept of that charge, some of them were encouraged and constrained to cast lot for it, and so he to whose lot it fell to be the Swede, had likewise his drum appointed, wherewith he did also levy his soldiers, but could but get some few more than fifty; all which nevertheless being bold boys, called themselves Swedes.

The next day (being Shrove Tuesday) the Swede with the sound of his drum and fifes, and flying colours went out of the town, through the gate called Sandgate, and went to his sconce, when having expected almost three hours, Tilly marched forth through the same gate with his troops, accompanied by many burghers and priests that did encourage them.

The Swede having given order to his soldiers came straight against Tilly, and put him presently to flight and so got the field. But some did encourage Tilly and persuaded him and his troops to gather again and set upon the Swedes, when the Swede made such an order among his company, that everyone did marvel at it, and so the second conflict the Swede got again the victory, took Tilly prisoner, and having bound him carried him into the town before his father's house, where he received some little money for his ransom.

But the day following, the reformators came to school, and caused the Swedes (as many as there were of those boys that had seemed on that side) to be whipped in their presence. So much, that some of them were not able to sit afterwards, although before their war they had been brought to it by many fair promises; especially one, who had been ensign, and is son to the judge of this town, who himself hath written this from thence hither, hath been well paid for his courage. He that was the Swede hath saved himself by running away.

The Continuation of our Forraine Avisoes, no. 18
(1632), 12–13

35 The Leipzig Assembly, 1631

An English newspaper account of the Protestants' assembly at Leipzig in 1631.

The Diet of Leipzig, February 1631
Present:
    In person:
Electors of Saxony, Brandenburg
Dukes John William and Bernhard of Saxe-Weimar
Landgrave William of Hesse-Cassel
Margrave Frederick of Baden-Durlach

Fürst August of Anhalt
Count Frederick of Solms
Counts John George and Ernest Louis of Mansfeld
 The [deposed] dukes of Mecklenburg.
    By representative:
Ducal Saxony, Pfalz-Zweibrücken, Brunswick-Lüneburg
[Protestant] members of the Circles of Swabia and Franconia
Ecclesiastical [Protestant] representatives of the abbess of Quedlinburg
Administrators of Magdeburg and Bremen
Counts of Stolberg
Lords of Reuss and Schönberg
Imperial towns of Nürnberg, Strassburg, Frankfurt am Main, Lübeck and Bremen
Other towns – Brunswick, Hildesheim, Mühlhausen, Nordhausen

Also present: Gustavus Adolphus's ambassador, Dr Chemnitz, and the vice-chancellor of the dukes of Württemberg.
Led by the Elector of Saxony.

And these be the Protestant party in the Empire some whereof being Lutherans, and some Calvinists; they first of all agree to have that distinction of names (which had caused so much schism and hatred heretofore) to be utterly taken away; making a general decree, that both professions should from thenceforth be called by one name of EVANGELICALS. That is, professors of the Gospel.

No man was suffered to stay within the town, whose business was not known: the streets ends were chained up and barricaded; guards set at the several ports; and the keys of the gates every night brought into the duke's chamber. And all this was to prevent spies and surprisals. . . .

The grievances of the Protestant Imperial Estates sent by the Elector of Saxony to Emperor Ferdinand II and to the Imperial Estates of the Catholic League, Leipzig 1631.

The cities and Circles of the Empire complain, that undue and excessive impositions and taxes have been laid upon them: not by the consent of themselves (as the Imperial laws command) but at the pleasure of any of the Emperor's commissaries. That under colour of protecting them, they have been forced to afford quarter and maintenance, unto the Imperial armies: who when they should indeed have defended them, most cowardly ran away. That when they would not endure the soldiers insolences, they have been declared enemies of the Empire, and forbidden to defend themselves. *That their lands have been given to soldiers, as if they had been conquered.*

That they have been forced to contribute to imaginary companies of Soldiers (perchance to four or five) as if they had been a complete band. That the commissaries have assigned quarters and passages unto the soldiers, without ever asking leave of the Princes or countries. That people have been tortured for their money, had their cattle driven away, their houses fired, and all commerce driven out of their country. *That the soldiers neither observed martial discipline, nor moral honesty*: neither keeping the laws, nor fearing God. That virgins and women have been ravished, upon the high altars. That if *weekly contributions* were not paid at the commissaries' absolute pleasure, the soldiers then spoiled the country.

The marquess of Brandenburg complains, that notwithstanding the king of Sweden had two parts of his country [the old and the new mark] yet was he forced to pay a full contribution, for the whole marquisate. That himself, by the soldiers so long lying in his country, was left so poor, that he was not able to entertain a garrison for the defence of his own palace: and was fain to abridge even the necessary provisions of his own table and family. That the soldiers entertained by the Protestants for their own defence, have been turned against them, to take away the church lands. That *treble* more contributions have been raised against no enemy, then ever were when the *Turk* was in Germany.

That when the princes of the house of Saxony, as namely, Altenberg, Weimar, and Coburg, had excused themselves of disability to pay each of them 1,451 dollars a month, which the Commissary Ossa had requested of them; then Tilly threatened to fetch 10,000 dollars a month out of them.

That considering all this, they could perceive nothing else, but that the Emperor had intended their utter ruin: whereas he had dealt more gently with those of his own hereditary dominions. That all this is most contrary unto the oath of the Emperor, and unto the laws of the Empire: and for such, hath been complained upon, by the several Electors and Princes; and by them protested against *in the late Diet of Ratisbon*. Wherefore they now humbly petition to be relieved, protesting otherwise, that they are no longer able to endure it: but shall be enforced to defend their persons, *the consciences*, their estates and subjects. Resolving notwithstanding to continue their due loyalty and obedience unto the Emperor. . . .

Leipzig, 18 March, 1631.

Conclusions of the Diet of Leipzig [February–March 1631]

1   That considering it was their sins which deserved these punishments; they command public prayers to be made to Almighty God for the averting of these miseries.

2   That means might be thought upon, and a friendly treaty appointed with the Catholic Princes, for removing of all jealousies, and restoring of good terms and concord betwixt them, as for seventy years before it had been.

3   That when the time and place for this treaty were once appointed; the Protestants should there appear a little before, to prepare themselves what to say in it.

4   And the fairlier to dispose both Caesar and the Catholics unto their intentions; that their grievances should in humble manner be beforehand by letter presented, both unto the Emperor and the *three* Catholic Electors.

5   That these grievances should in those letters be pressed; to be contrary unto the Emperor's oath, the Imperial laws, the privileges of the Princes, the honour and safety of the Empire. That the wars would undo all, the insolences of commissaries and soldiers were so insufferable, as that it stood neither with their consciences, their safeties, nor their honours, to suffer themselves and subjects, to be any longer thus abused; and that they would hereupon desire the benefit of the Emperor's so often promised protection.

6   That seeing these greater and fuller assemblies were both chargeable and tedious; they agreed that certain deputies should as necessity required be in the names of all the rest appointed, both to treat and determine of what should seem convenient for the common cause.

7   They decree of levies of soldiers (both of horse and foot) to be made in their several dominions and divisions: without crossing the constitutions of the Empire, or offence of any; and only in their own defence.

8   That whereas in a diet of the Empire held 1555 it had been decreed how that neighbouring Princes should live neighbourly, and if any oppressed others, the rest should relieve them; this relief they now promise one another; desiring that if in these troublesome times, the levies and other carriages could not possibly be every way agreeable to the constitutions of the Empire that it might not be interpreted to be done of purpose.

9   They decree the continuance of their loyalty and obedience unto His Imperial Majesty.

10   *They agree also upon the proportion of the levies*:
Elector of Saxony – 6 regiments. Brandenburg – 3 regiments.
Circles of Swabia, Rhine, Franconia – 3 each.
Circle of Lower Saxony – money in lieu of 1 regiment.
Each regiment – 3,000 foot and 1,000 horse

And thus the Diet being ended upon Palm Sunday [1631] with a
sermon; Saxony displayed his defensive banner, beats up his drums,
begins his levies; and so at their coming home, do the rest of the Princes.

The Swedish Intelligencer, 1 (1632), Cambridge
University Library, Acton.d.sel.601, 22 ff.

36   Chronicle interpretation

A seventeenth-century chronicle and its nineteenth-century interpretation.

Text
The old church records of Ummerstadt, an agricultural town near
Coburg, famed, from olden times, throughout the country for its good
pottery, report as follows:

Although in the year 1632 the whole country, as also the said little
town, was very populous, so that it alone contained more than 150
citizens, and up to 800 souls, yet from the ever-continuing war troubles,
and the constant quartering of troops, the people became in such-wise
enervated, that from great and incessant fear, a pestilence sent upon us by
the all-powerful and righteous God, carried off as many as 500 men in the
years 1635 and 1636; on account of this lamentable and miserable
condition of the time, no children were born into the world in the course
of two years. Those whose lives were still prolonged by God Almighty,
have from hunger, the dearness of the times, and the scarcity of precious
bread, eaten and lived upon bran, oil-cakes, and linseed husks, and many
have also died of it; many also have been dispersed over all countries,
most of whom have never again seen their dear fatherland.

In the year 1640, during the Saalfeld encampment, Ummerstadt
became a city of the dead or of shadows; for during 18 weeks no man
dared to appear therein, and all that remained was destroyed. Therefore
the population became quite thin, and there were not more than 100
souls forthcoming. [In 1850 the place had 893 inhabitants.]

Interpretation
Monotonously did the death wail sound in the chronicles and records of
fellow-sufferers. Where thousands were saved, millions were ruined and
destroyed. There was destruction of house, wealth and life, alike in town

and country. Manifold was the work of the destroying forces, but a higher force was unceasingly at work to ward off final ruin.

Even in the time of the king of Sweden many villages were entirely abandoned, the beasts of the woods roamed about among the blackened rafters, and perhaps the tattered figure of some old bedlame or cripple might be seen. From that time ruin increased to such an extent, that nothing like it can be found in modern history. To the destructive demons of the sword were added others, not less fearful and still more voracious. The land was little cultivated and the harvest was bad. An unheard-of rise in prices ensued, famine followed, and in the years 1635 and 1636 a pestilence attacked the enfeebled population, more terrible than had raged for more than a century in Germany. It spread its pass slowly over the whole of Germany, over the soldier as well as over the peasant, armies were dissipated under its parching breath, many places lost their inhabitants, and in some villages in Franconia and Thuringia there remained only a few individuals.

> G. Freytag, *Pictures of German Life* II (London, 1862), 86, 117–18, 198

37 'The Tears of Germany', 1638

The sermon was an important form of mass communication. The following extract from a Lutheran sermon in Nuremberg, 1638, adds a certain xenophobia of its own to the popular view of war horrors.

Our dear country, that was once so rich, so full of plenty, so abounding with multitudes of people, so glorious for arts, so renowned for pleasantness, for strength, for our many, great and beautiful cities, for our large and graceful churches, for variety of all worldly delights. . . . What relief has our superfluity and plenty of things afforded to those that have been in want? What afflicted churches have not tasted of Germany's liberality? Witness the relief and succour that English divines have found among us; witness Denmark, Poland, France, Spain, Italy. . . . What a bulwark and defence has it been against the common adversaries of Christians; what famous sieges has Germany endured for the defence of the Gospel. . . . What country has outstripped her (O fair beloved Germany) in any excellencies or privileges?

But these times are gone; oh, how my soul mourns to see her excellence thus departed. . . . Where shall I begin to reckon up her troubles? What shall I say of the lamentable extortions and exactions upon all Estates? What shall I say of the tortures and torments inflicted upon people of each status, sex and age? What shall I insist upon the rapes and ravishings, without distinction of persons or places, unfit to be rehearsed? What need I relate the robberies, pillagings, plunderings of villages, cities, against promises and public oaths? What shall I say of the murders and bloodshed committed on every acre of ground in our land? What need I to insist upon the general devastations by fire in every region as the armies have marched? You are all witnesses. . . . The sword has not marched without other judgements to accompany it, as heavy or heavier than itself; as fire, famine, pestilence; and has not yet blunted, but is moving on as furiously as if it had scarcely begun its work.

Elton, 246–7

38 'The German Brutus', 1636

The German Brutus: that is, a letter thrown before the public.

The states and cities of the Empire, so long as they were in your hands, contributed fully and sufficiently to your maintenance; many, nay too many, to say the least of it, as a proof of their fidelity, have lost soul and body, wealth and life, nay all their privileges, and, in a great measure, religion itself.

Regensburg testifies to this. Augsburg laments over it. All grieve together over it. You have allowed the old regiments to dissolve, have completed no companies, nor paid either new or old, notwithstanding you have demanded, and in fact received large sums of money from many diets; I say nothing of what you have extorted from your enemies in their own countries.

How has this money been spent? In superfluous pomp and luxury which is hateful to everyone. We have observed this silently, and made a virtue of necessity. The children of Israel, when they had intercourse with the daughters of their enemies, and afterwards boasted of their victory, and tormented their brethren of Judah with the hardest yoke of bondage, were both times severely punished by God. And shall it fare better with you who have exercised more than Turkish cruelty in many evangelical places?

The corn from the monastery of Magdeburg, the dukedom of Brunswick and other places, has been threshed out and carried off in heaps from the country, sold at a very high price and the money spent for your own use, nothing given to the poor soldiers; the country people, harassed to death, are dying of hunger; and many fortresses from avarice, either not supplied with provisions, or not provided with powder and shot and, in short, general mismanagement.

Now we see for ourselves everywhere abandoned by fortune, so that at last we discover there is no money in hand, and no people to be got, as those who are available have run away, and the remainder will no longer be restrained by martial law. . . . 'When the Prince leads the life of Lucifer, what wonder that his subjects become devils.'

Freytag II, 152–3

39   Cannibalism at Breisach, 1638

This account comes from a fly-sheet, 'News concerning the great famine and emergency that arose during the siege of Breisach', printed in 1639 (see above, p. xvi for a note on coinage and measures).

On 9 December [1638] Breisach surrendered . . . after a siege that started on 18 August. The famine in Breisach during this time was as follows.

At first a sester of wheat cost 8 ducats and it was even traded against a fur coat valued at 40 reichstalers. A woman paid for a sester of wheat with a jewel worth 40 ducats. Rye went for 9 gulden and barley at 4 ducats. Finally a sester of oats went for 50 gulden and linseed 9 gulden. Even rough husks cost 8 gulden. One hundred gulden was paid for a metzen of bran. A baker could made 132 gulden worth of 'bread' out of 5 litres of bran, and a sester of corn yielded 50 reichstalers. Bran bread retailed at 18 batzen for the pound. Real bread cost 3 gulden and 2 schilling for the pound. A pound of fat bacon cost 1 reichstaler. A pound of butter was 4 gulden: a pound of horsemeat 5 schilling: a pound of unrinsed horse innards and a hand's breadth of tripe cost 8 schilling. A horse's hoof fetched 5 schilling and a pound of dog 5 batzen. Many mice and rats were sold at high prices. An egg cost 1 gulden and a chicken 5 gulden. A turnip was 2 gulden and a pound of salt 12 batzen. A pound of kale made 1 gulden and 30 kreuzer, and even a cabbage cost 6 kreuzer. A quarter of a pound of veal was sold at 8 gulden. Nearly all the dogs and cats were eaten. Several thousand horses, cows, oxen, calves and sheep were consumed.

On 24 November a soldier under arrest in the prison died, and before the warder in charge could order his burial the other prisoners had taken the body, cut it up and eaten it. The prisoners even picked holes into the walls of their prison with their fingers and ate what they found. Two corpses were dug up and cut open. The innards were taken out and eaten. In one day three children were consumed.

The soldiers promised a pastry-cook's boy a piece of bread if he followed them to camp. But when he got there, they cut him up and ate him. On 10 December eight well known burghers' children alone disappeared in the fishers' district, presumed eaten, since they could never be traced, not to mention all the children of beggars and strangers whom no one knew anyway. In the town square alone ten corpses were found, not counting all those found in the alleys and on the dung-heaps.

On 12 December another prisoner died and before the warder in charge could have him buried, the other prisoners fell onto the corpse and tore at it with their teeth, eating the raw flesh. A cavalry captain saw how a sester of hemp-seed went for 26 reichstalers and that is what the poor had to pay in order to survive. Before 1 January a calf cost 26 reichstalers. On the last day before the defenders marched out, a bowl of sauerkraut went for a golden ring. Several people lived for three, four and up to five weeks on warm water and salt only. But their hands and feet swelled up and they died. Seven imprisoned Swedish soldiers were eaten.

Is this not a great calamity above all miseries that one should hear of this and watch partly similar happenings every year, month, week, day and hour?

> No wonder that we're dying,
> when such atrocities
> are God's punishment to Germany, as alas,
> I have myself experienced
> from youth 'til now
> in my married years,
> as is clearly manifest
> in what I have suffered.
> Yet God shall never forsake me.
> He helps me through the harshest times,
> through many fights and great conflicts,
> in war emergency and plague,
> on the open field and on the frontier.
> I thank you, Jesus Christ,
> my helper always,
> who from many perils saved me,
> and helped me through hard times
> with scoundrels, who are everywhere
> to pain the honest folk
> with their godless living
> and striving against God's order.
> Oh, true God, unmask their deeds;
> build a defence against this false band,
> who destroy your Holy Word

in many places.
Stay with us, O Lord above,
and we will always praise you;
on your heavenly throne
hear me, Lord, through your Son.
I wish for nothing more,
here and now, 'amen', I say with all my heart.
My name is Hans Heberle,
Now God give me eternal joy.
                                        Heberle, 175–7

PART II SOCIAL IMPACT

The war years witnessed an endless series of guerilla campaigns between peasants and soldiers (**40, 41–2**). Soldiers were peasants in arms, and peasants became soldiers in arms. Indiscriminate recruitment was practised by all the larger territorial governments at some stage during the period. This meant that large numbers of *déracinés* from village and town fed on the land and, like locusts, died when all the food, clothing and shelter had been consumed within their radius of action (**39, 40, 44–5**). There was no immediate demobilization of troops (**50**), although much more research has yet to be done on this aspect of the final stages of the war. On the whole, soldiers suffered as cruelly as peasants, whereas officers, townsmen and clergy who usually had access to private means, education and the law, and to walled cities or forts, suffered much less. Their tales of woe usually concerned the fate of others (**59**). Where they were directly affected themselves, they wasted no effort in lamenting the fact in great detail (**60**), although these times of emergency could also make the careers of those who responded to the challenge by emerging as local saviours (**58**). Naturally, towns could fare badly in the hands of the enemy (**53**), whereas one's own troops usually limited themselves to pillaging the villages, since towns could more readily retaliate at law and in politics.

Military commanders, however mercenary, failed to establish themselves permanently as successful new dynasts, dictators or despots. Wallenstein was no early example of Bonaparte, and Bernhard of Saxe-Weimar certainly failed where a much later swashbuckler like Bernadotte was to succeed. Furthermore, those dynastic and territorial rulers who were displaced as a result of rivalries, religion or rebellion nearly all returned or at least their descendants returned to the inheritance. The war years only succeeded in reaffirming the traditional, legal-dynastic and feudal structure of governing society. It made fools of many grand nobles and territorial rulers (**66–9**) but seemed once more to retrench the ruling ranks and orders of society much in the same way as it retrenched the early modern German federal system of politics in the Empire. On the face of it the Thirty Years War may indeed have taken religion out of politics, and it may indeed have established an international, *ad hoc* European balance of power, yet it was not a total war of the sort we know from the twentieth century. It produced no immediate, drastic social changes and no major revolutionary, democratic or technological advances. What it did produce was bureaucratic and fiscal proliferation of state power, grinding down all the more harshly any independent Estates' and peasant-artisan development in politics, law, local government and labour relations, in the interest of absolutism and its expert manipulators – officialdom.

The equation, war equals social progress, does not readily seem to apply to the era of the Thirty Years War in Germany. However, what may apply more readily is that war equals bureaucratic and fiscal proliferation at the expense of real social progress, which when bottled up has become explosive, as can be seen in subsequent major wars and revolutions. Our period of study may be seen as an example of social stagnation combined with great advances in state power. This is the real problem of the 'general crisis of the seventeenth century', and for Europe the Germany of the Thirty Years War may be seen to lie at the heart of it.

IV Peasants and soldiers

40 The experience of a Bavarian monastery and its village, 1633

As told by Maurus Friesenegger, monk and then abbot at Andechs.

On 30 September [1633] another troop of one thousand Imperial Spanish cavalry passed through. Although as new recruits they understood no military discipline, they did understand blackmail and robbery, whereat the inhabitants once more left house and home and fled into the woods. On the same day, since the Augsburgers knew that the whole of Bavaria was bereft of troops, and because they were driven on by hunger, for the Croats had long ago scoured the countryside, they overran the town of Landsberg, plundered it for four days, molesting the inhabitants fearfully and returning home to Augsburg with their booty. Three hundred of them came to Peiting in order to ambush the Croats and massacre them to be rid of them. But since many of them were only interested in booty and since the rest fled, they took up their baggage and horses with the help of the peasants, with whom the Croats were more hated than the Swedes because of their thieving. The Croats, however, gave chase and killed about 15 of the Augsburgers. The rest reached Landsberg with their booty.

On 1 October we once again heard the fearful news that the Swedes had broken in and were plundering and laying waste to the village inn. At Inning they stole four horses. Afterwards the rumour went around that the thieves were Imperial troops.

In the night one could see first two then six fearful fires burning in the Lechrain towards Augsburg, lasting for another day and night, from which it was concluded that the Swedes from Augsburg were laying waste everything as they thought there were no more soldiers to resist them in Bavaria. All was prepared for flight once more, in the monastery just as at the village of Erling, where the church was just being reconsecrated. Yet it was thought advisable first to get to the truth of the matter. A man was sent over the lake to Stegen to look into the situation. He returned with the welcome news that Imperial troops had caught the Augsburg Swedes near Landsberg as they were returning with booty, waylaying them at night in Prittriching, and taking all their horses and booty, pursuing them beyond Bergen and Kissing with serious losses to the enemy. Booty and horses have been taken via Stegen to Munich. How large the booty and losses inflicted on the enemy could never be fully ascertained. Once the Imperial and Bavarian troops, who were not very numerous, had returned, the enemy also reappeared and in revenge burnt down 140 houses in the parish of Prittriching, in Bergen all but two small houses, 40 in Mering, nine in Kissing and an unknown number of thatches and houses. After the event the story was put out that Colonel Sperreuther had invaded Bavaria with 3,000 Swedes, plundered Landsberg and its environs, setting up his headquarters at Prittriching, and that an arquebusier detachment of cavalry belonging to General Johann von Werth had made a night raid on his headquarters, captured up to 400 horses along with all the baggage, burning whatever could not be carried away, killing a first lieutenant, a cavalry captain, an ensign and several other officers. Colonel Sperreuther fled on foot into a marsh, where pursuing horsemen lost track of him in the dark.

On 13 October during the first service after reconsecration of Erling village church the alarm was raised several times, whereat many people ran out of the church. But only five cavalrymen appeared, asking for fodder. There was lively coming and going of troops for a long while, although it never cost the villagers too much, but something was always demanded.

At this time the diocese consecrated many vessels and chalices of tin, sending them into the parishes where not only the churches had been plundered, but where the altars had also been desecrated. Notwithstanding this, there was often shortage of wine, wafers and other necessities so that the mass had to be cancelled, especially as the parish clergy often had no supplies and not even enough black bread to eat.

On 23 October the abbot came back to Heiligenberg [Holy Mountain] monastery, bringing with him the Elector of Saxony who was a prisoner of war in Munich. [This report is inaccurate.]

On 1 November we received through the post the sad news that the Swedes had captured Neuburg and that they now intended to attack Bavaria once more to our final destruction. We also heard from Munich that soldiers were being recruited to fight against the enemy near Aichbach.

On 6 November before dawn a messenger came running from Herrsching, and warned us that in the night 20 riders had entered Herrsching, driven the inhabitants out with shovels, broken open doors and stolen among other things three horses and several head of cattle. After inflicting a number of wounds on an old man, they shot him dead. Everyone thought that they were Swedes but it later turned out that they were Imperial troops [i.e. Catholic troops who were supposed to be defending the Bavarian inhabitants from the Protestant Swedes].

On 19 November Regensburg went over to the Swedes in large part due to the heretical [i.e. Protestant] citizens who refused to defend the city. This caused even greater fear in Bavaria.

On 22 November we were warned several times that billets would be commandeered, since 3,000 cavalry from Alsace were on the move to join Johann von Werth. Once again the whole village of Erling fled into the woods, leaving all the houses empty. The cavalry marched via Starnberg, however, and Erling was spared, although all the places in the vicinity such as Pocking, Traubing, Frieding and so on, were occupied. They suffered considerable damage.

On 26 November 20 riders appeared. They were thieves, content, however, to accept a few handfuls of oats, but not without threats since the peasants had gathered around them in strength.

Even in December despite an uncommonly cold spell of weather we had no peace. Down at Straubing the Swedes under the duke of Weimar [Bernhard of Saxe-Weimar] robbed, burnt and murdered wherever they went. Up here in our district 30 horsemen or thieves consisting of Croats and Poles went from place to place doing much the same. They had been ordered to keep the Augsburgers in check, to cut all their lines of supply and keep any marauding Swedes at bay. However, they merely showed the Augsburgers and Swedes how to do it all the more brutally.

On 5 December they attacked Brunnen, stole horses, cattle and whatever appealed to them. They shot dead the parish priest, Johann Huter, since he had refused to give them his horses without further ado.

On 9 December the Augsburgers raided Fürstenfeld monastery and the market of Bruck, taking a great amount of booty as well as five or six monks as hostages to Augsburg, one of whom was clad only in a shirt despite the severe cold.

On 12 December they made another sortie and harried the Lech valley, burning down a number of houses at Scheuring along with its two churches. They took some peasants prisoner and that aroused great fear and horror throughout the whole region.

On 14 December a fisherman returning from Stegen explained that a number of horsemen had arrived there and asked how far it was to the Holy Mountain, how far to Seefeld, Diessen, Weilheim and if the abbot and baron were in residence. That led us to consider and to prepare for flight once more.

On 18 December two riders appeared with written orders confirming that they were to be quartered with us for our own safety and they became our defence unit or *salva guardia*, since the whole body of our army was soon expected to pass out of Alsace into Bavaria, taking up headquarters at Weilheim and Schongau. Whatever any subject wished to rescue was to be taken into the monastery since safety could not be guaranteed everywhere. Thus the monastery once more became a common stable and cowshed, a depository for the remaining goods of the common subjects and a refectory for men, women and children.

The inhabitants of Machtlfing and Traubing soon experienced what our *salva guardia* had meant. Freebooters stole ten horses from Machtlfing and after ransoming them back to the villagers for 23 gulden they still made off with the four best horses. In Traubing they took the ransom plus all the horses.

Since the people of several villages had all fled into the monastery, the women and children were assigned places in the outer buildings. But owing to the severe weather they went into the monastery to get warm. The men barricaded the corridors with beams, armed themselves with a variety of firearms and stones in order to defend the monastery and their few possessions against small bands of thieves.

On 19 December 14 riders and robbers passed through Erling. As they found nothing in the village they captured a number of army supply units [*Marketender*] proceeding across the fields towards camp. Money and goods to the value of 4,000 gulden were stolen. We were fortunate in having our *salva guardia* to prove that we had not perpetrated the crime. In the night 50 armed peasants went from Seefeld to Aschering where they ambushed a den of thieves who had earlier that day stolen five horses from the Seefelders on the road near Munich. The peasants shot dead the leader of the robbers and put the rest to flight, taking their horses home with them.

On 20 December more than 20 riders reappeared outside the monastery and demanded food, drink and fodder. Our *salva guardia* turned them down and since they commanded little respect, we called for our armed peasants, whereat the riders went away. And the whole day long riders appeared. To several people who were on foot and who begged rather than demanded, we gave beer and bread. At nightfall two important riders appeared and demanded a present from the colonel in return for his *salva guardia*. We sent him a stag but for the rest we excused ourselves out of poverty. Immediately after this we received an urgent message from Generalissimo Altringer from Dettenschwang, demanding three or four mounted men who knew the whole area between the Ammer and Wurm lakes, since he wished to pass through here on the following day with his whole army.

On 21 December at about nine o'clock in the morning the troops marched through and they kept coming until nightfall. Cavalry, infantry, ordnance and baggage followed one after the other and from Erling each was assigned a billet in the surrounding villages. Some greeted the Holy Mountain from afar and others visited the shrine where they paid for beer and bread, also giving alms generously. But the common soldiers gave our *salva guardia* much trouble. The latter were finally able to cope with them, although they behaved badly in the village where stoves and windows were smashed just to show who was now master in the house, especially when they could find no food. Even more troops passed through Stegen. After nightfall there was real misery. The last to march through were the Spaniards, and to make matters worse, they were infantry too. One thousand and five hundred of them stayed in the village of Erling, making camp and resting until the third day. The monastery provided lodging for two colonels who were Spanish counts, plus their servants. The former were content with two rooms and very little food, beer and bread. Anything above this they offered to pay for. They alone were to eat free of charge but their servants could hardly be satisfied, commandeering everything with force and paying with rough behaviour. They also demanded stabling and fodder for four horses but it turned out to be for 20.

The village, where the soldiers found only empty houses and no people, became a terrible sight. The whole village seemed to be aflame. They took chairs and benches out of the houses, removed roofs, filling the streets with dangerous camp-fires and the whole village echoed to their shouts and screams that could only have been brought on by hunger and despair. Not a single villager who looked on from afar had any hope of seeing his house again when the next day dawned.

On the following day the starving soldiers searched the woods and found enough that had been hidden to still their hunger and misery. Anyone they met on the road or in the fields they deprived of clothes, shoes and socks, sending them away in snow, ice and severe cold.

On 22 December these monsters burnt down the beautiful castle of Mühlfeld. They piled up tables and chairs and set it alight. Some of them who had wished to put the fire out were threatened to be shot by the rest. Father Kellerer from the monastery quickly arrived at the scene with the *salva guardia* as well as a number of Spaniards and peasants. He could not rescue the church, tower and chapel. Since we intended to make a complaint about the damage to their general, the duke a Feria, we had first of all to prepare a document exonerating our colonels from all blame. Such was then sent to a Feria at Starnberg, and he passed it on to Generalissimo Altringer at headquarters in Perchting. From there a reply came back to our colonels. One of them was ordered to move out of the monastery and take up quarters in the village with a strict order to keep closer watch over the safety of the monastery. This colonel now became our enemy and we had to ask his superiors once more for permission to keep him lodged in the monastery.

After we had once more waited impatiently for the 23 December to arrive [when the Spaniards were expected to move on] we received orders that they would stay longer since no winter quarters had been made ready for them. Himmel! Soldiers and peasants were now to be seen half clothed and pale with misery, emaciated with hunger and walking about with bare feet in the great cold. What would happen in the long term? The soldiers were eating dogs, cats and any stolen meat. For days on end the peasants had not even a crust of bread. Many searched our monastery garden for greens, winter lettuce, roots and herbs, which they then ate raw or stewed. The army sent to Munich for provisions and in the monastery we slaughtered the cattle and baked bread for as many people as possible. Bakers from as far afield as Diessen as well as others also supplied us with bread. But what help was that against so many? There were 1,500 soldiers in the village and inside the monastery the population of several other places, too. Since the suppliers of provisions were often robbed with violence of their money on the way and of their goods on the return journey, they soon gave up. So hunger increased greatly among the soldiers and even the officers began to feel something, as hard cash no longer bought anything.

On 28 December those who were starving broke into the Church of Our Dear Lady in the village and climbed under the roof removing the seed-corn stored there for next spring. Thus disappeared the last hope of the peasants.

On 30 December the troops of the foreign and Spanish regiments mustered, and it proved to be quite a spectacle. There were half-filled companies of blackened and jaundiced faces, starved bodies, half clothed or bedecked in rags and stolen clothing of women. It was the face of hunger and famine. Next to them the officers appeared well fed and elegantly dressed. Many soldiers were ill and many also died of starvation and cold to the extent that their regimental priest had to hear the

confession of 30 of them in one day alone. And that is what death – the
end of all evils, fears and hopes – did to us.

> Maurus Friesenegger, *Tagebuch aus dem*
> *dreissigjährigen Krieg. Nach einer Handschrift im*
> *Kloster Andechs*, edited by W. Mathäser
> (Munich, 1974), 49–59

41   Rebellious peasants in the Land above the Enns, 1626

In 1626 the Lutheran region around Linz in Upper Austria rebelled against the
troops of its provisional ruler, Catholic Maximilian I of Bavaria. The town was
besieged by rebels in July and August and then again, especially in November. An
anonymous, possibly even pro-Lutheran broadside relates the story after the
collapse of an earlier uprising. The narrator is made out to be a spurious Italian
haberdasher, who is writing home in pidgin 'German'.

Dearest Signor,

Your note, number 1, of 27 October has been received in our Lutheran
[*luderisch* or dissolute] Land at Linz. By the Devil, I hear that in our Italy,
where there are many Catholic priests and beautiful whores, this year's
crops of oranges, lemons, citrons and everything else have been very
good. I'm glad to hear it. They would soon make you run away, by God,
for here in Upper Austria there are many Lutheran peasants who are
never of good intent, by the Devil. The peasant, the mousehead, has
become as rebellious as a thousand devils. On the holy day when God
ascended to heaven, they have suddenly run all over the land – ratt-a-tatt-
tatt, run.

O Signor, I cannnot write how the Lutheran rascals behaved, of how
they slew our pious priests until they were stretched out on all fours. They
are rebellious mouseheads indeed. Run like the devil. But our lord,
Count Hebersdorff [Maximilian's governor] poured a dish of hot soup
over them until the hair of the Lutheran beasts was burned off their heads,
by the Devil.

[The author then relates how the peasants deprived him of his wares
and asks for more to be sent from Italy.]

But the Lutheran whore in Upper Austria does not want to buy any
more spindles. So send me a couple of pieces of double-taffeta so that I
can make the Lutherans pay.

When I think of the Lutheran thieves I go mad. When they wanted to
kill me, they would have stabbed me with my stiletto, good Signor. But
when they could not stand the smell [of gunpowder], the Lutheran rascals
ran quickly to Wels. There, Pappenheim [Hebersdorff's son-in-law and

Imperialist-Leaguist general] with his cavalry met the Lutheran beasts and cut them down like dogs. Then they ran like a thousand devils.

Now the land is too cramped for the rascals. They do not know where to go, and the Emperor now will ask:

Ay, Lutheran mousehead, where is it, your letter of privilege from your royal master? Has it not been thrown in the open sewer, where so much stink has come into it. Where are your privileges now? It stinks. They must come now to be hanged and to be decapitated over the whole country. And the Lutheran mousehead must flee like any common criminal.

But the Catholic soldiers are cutting their heads off like lice running off your head. And you are getting what you deserve from them. Why did they get rebellious? If only they had not slain Catholic priests and soldiers; if only Catholic priests and soldiers had not slain them.

Well now, Signor Francesco, you know how things are here in Upper Austria and I am serene in God when I think of the Lutheran beasts. I can't write better now.

Farewell Signor, greet my dear equals who were sent to the galleys in Venice, and my dear friends all our peasants.

From Linz, where in the town-ditch so many Lutheran peasants lie buried, and above.

To all our friends,

Signor Francesco Spazagamini

Give this good messenger a tip.

> British Library, Print Room, Foreign History. Translation adapted from E. A. Beller, *Propaganda in Germany during the Thirty Years War* (Princeton, 1940), plate VIII. For discussion, see Amt der oberösterreichischen Landesregierung (ed.), *Der oberösterreichische Bauernkrieg 1626* (Linz, 1976), 1–172, especially 11

42   Peasant retaliation against the Swedes in South Germany, 1632

A report in the London press from Augsburg, 12 May 1632.

This day the king of Sweden breaks up with his army from Landshut. . . .

The whole bishopric of Freisingen is freely yielded up to His Majesty and paid him contribution. Hereupon some boors in Swaben being 10,000 strong have assembled themselves together, they have taken again

Leutkirch and Wangen, they have with them some pieces of ordnance. But some of our forces which are already sent against them will soon cool their courage.

This week the afore mentioned boors did overcome and surprise 50 Swedish soldiers. Crabates, between Schrobenhousen and Sticha, these boors when they had mastered them, did cut off their ears and noses, chopped off their hands and feet, and put out their eyes, and so left them, these devilish boors do great mischief of the like nature.

As soon as the king of Sweden was advertised of the cruell insolencies of these boors he was much displeased, and so much the more because he saw that his soldiers would not put it up but presently cried revenge and fired their villages, insomuch that in one day there were seen 200 several fires blazing at once.

> 'The Continuation of our Weekly News', *Forraine Avisoes*, no. 26 London, 6 June 1632, for N. Butter and N. Bourne, Cambridge University Library, Syn.7.64. 123 2, 4

43   The weather, prophecy and prayer

In the year 1624, from Christmas until 2 February, it was a cold, hard winter so that there was a real shortage of water. Then around the first night of Lent rain came, melting the snow and lively spring set in. It was as if summer had come and the dear corn started to show green on the fields. Then God came again around 8, 9, 10 March with severe weather of a kind that we have never seen in the deepest wintertime with snow, wind and cold. But it did not stay long and it was soon milder. In March corn was 9 gulden in good money, rye 7 gulden and oats 4 gulden [to the imen]. . . .

On 13 July the false prophet became a liar. What he had foretold was as follows [based on a fly-sheet circulating in Ulm at that time]. In July of 1638, on the 13th according to the old and on the 23rd according to the new calendar, a Friday, just as the sun moves into the house of the lion there will be a terribly violent storm with hail, lightning and heavy thunderclaps with wind and wondrous signs. And around midday the sun will lose its light and the moon will appear in great fright whereat many people will of their own accord out of fear cast themselves from high places and towers. A fearful, cruel wind will be heard accompanied by earth tremors which will overthrow not only the great palaces, towers, churches and massive trees, but will even uproot and cast them down. Voices like those of human beings will be heard and it will put mighty fear into all cattle and animals who will howl in return. Above all, these events will occur abroad in Italy at Sicily, Mantua, Venice, Florence, Rome, and also at Prague and at home in Ulm in Swabia and other places. In the night before the Friday human voices and animal noises will be heard and in the firmament of heaven there shall appear a fiery comet, not very large but in the shape of a fiery sword. In the same night between five and six o'clock all the rivers, wells and the sea will overflow and flood the land so that many buildings and houses with people will be destroyed.

Then in these same wells poisoned animals and water flukes will appear. Finally between seven and eight at night the fearful earthquake will cause gruesome damage and destroy all the buildings especially those of high and wealthy people and this will go on for 22 hours.

The truth of this is namely that the person who has made this prophecy had successfully predicted the recent earthquake in Italy where a thousand places were destroyed with great material damage. May God be merciful to us. This man and prophet is said to have been put into prison at Venice. If his prediction does not materialize, he is to have his head cut off.

But all this was lies, and all he succeeded in doing was to create havoc in a number of places. And many superstitious and foolish people wanted to flee from those places that he named as doomed.

On 22 July we cut the corn and the Ulm imen of corn stood at 6 gulden, rye at 3 gulden. By 28 July corn had come down to 5 gulden. On 30 July a battle took place outside Breisach. . . .

In a book [Arnold Mengering, *Perversa ultima seculi Militia oder Kriegs-Belial, Der Soldaten Teuffel*, second edition, Altenburg, 1638] at chapter 13 on page 257 I read about the hellish system of soldiers as they dealt with the Imperial city of Ulm. Around Ulm and in the upper part of Swabia 44 companies of cavalry and footsoldiers were billeted and more were expected to arrive at any minute. They behaved in a very arbitrary manner and totally ruined the countryside. The fine Imperial city of Ulm had to pay them war tax at the following rate *per week*:

15 cavalry captains, each at 75 fl, comes to	1,125 fl	
30 lieutenants, each at 37 fl 30 kr, comes to	1,025 fl	
30 ensigns, each at 30 fl, comes to	900 fl	
15 sergeants, each at 30 fl, comes to	450 fl	
1,500 riders, each 2 fl for drink, comes to	3,000 fl	
further for each, 3 quarters of oats for their horses, comes to, in money	2,625 fl	
further for each, 2 pounds of meat and 2 pounds of bread at 14 kreuzer, comes to	2,471 fl	20 kr

16 captains of foot, each at 30 fl, comes to	480 fl
16 lieutenants, each at 25 fl, comes to	320 fl
64 common officers and 5,000 soldiers per week	26,490 fl

Total per week, 39,736 fl 20 kr. [note the multiplication and adding mistakes]. . . .

Because of this dangerous state of war (*kriegsleuffen*) an hour of prayer has been decreed and instituted in town and country to pray to Almighty God for release from the present punishment and ask him to be good to us once more, in the year 1628 on the 12th day of May. [This hour of prayer was kept for 22 years until 3 September 1650, and it consisted of ten Biblical texts and ten psalms. Ulm city council also issued a printed version which sold for 2 kreuzers.]

Heberle, 111–12, 123–4, 172–3

44   Wallenstein orders the return of peasants' horses, 1625

Letter of Wallenstein to Collato, Halberstadt, 3 December 1625.

Coloredo has just sent word to me that his brother had told him to send 100 mounted musketeers to him. Since he has no horses, would I allow him to take horses from the peasants and turn them into riding horses? To this I replied that his evilly disciplined regiment had already caused far too much damage and disruption, and now I did not want them further to molest the peasants.

When the people who have taken the peasants' horses arrive, his brother will return the horses at once to the peasants. In no way is he to make use of them, but instead he must send me a list of the officers responsible, so that I can punish them severely.

Schulz I, 45

45   Maximilian of Bavaria warns against billeting, 1637

Billeting is such a burden for most unfortunate people that they can no longer put up with it, even if they have not suffered in any other way. Therefore the few still remaining, poor and oppressed subjects plead for redress in such lamentable circumstances, that it would make a stone feel compassion. Furthermore, one should only but leave them alone in their little hut in the raw winter with their poor little children to eat their acorn gruel to keep body and soul together, and not cause them to be driven from house and home through this great, unspeakable affliction, that makes them lie more wretchedly than game in the snow and woods, pitifully causing them and their children to die and rot of frost and hunger.

Thus I have not shirked my duty of obediently informing Your Majesty [Emperor Ferdinand III] of these miserable, long-term matters and afflictions once again with my own messenger, and to ask you to call a swift stop to the apportioning of winter quarters. . . .

The majority of the cavalry goes on foot. The poor soldiers are through and through paupers, stripped bare, exhausted, starved and in such a condition that it is easy to commiserate with them. They badly need nourishing provisions if one is to get active service out of them next spring.

Jessen, 377

46   A soldier is convicted for stealing, 1623

Judgement from a military court, 20 November 1623

The widow of the treasurer of Cottbus, Mrs Elisabetha Francken, domiciled in the Peiz, pleads that the following objects have been wickedly stolen from her house, and that after thorough enquiries she discovered that it was due to Hans Jacob von Pirchen, a young ensign of the late Hans von Gotz's company. While the ensign was billeted with Mrs Francken, he exchanged several talers and ducats, and when she examined them more closely, she discovered that they were her own coins. Whereupon the widow informed Captain Senff who immediately confronted Hans Jacob von Pirchen. . . . The latter admitted taking all that Mrs Francken had itemized, except for 2 ducats, 10 silver buttons and the man's shirts, all of which were returned to the widow excepting an amount the equivalent of 8 talers, which was not recovered.

Bearing in mind that Hans Jacob is still very young and has not yet come under full military discipline, nevertheless according to the regulations operated by the regimental sergeant-major, Captain Senff has been constrained to hold an impartial military trial to ascertain the truth of the deed. The court was filled with 12 properly sworn in officers and soldiers who were unanimous in finding the following judgement.

Although Hans Jacob is very young and not yet under full military discipline, nevertheless he has crudely sinned against the seventh commandment of God, and therefore he is condemned to death by hanging. However, it was further noted by the court that the criminal had not broken open the money chest, but that the defendant had left her keys in the lock of the chest and thereby tempted the criminal to commit the deed. As the old proverb says, 'opportunity makes a thief', and so because of this, the serious plea of mercy is considered justified. And unanimously they have asked His Electoral Highness to grant the offender mercy, since he is still so young, as well as being of noble descent, and thirdly because he was almost given cause to commit the crime, since the keys were left in the money chest in the first place. They are agreed that mercy should stand in place of justice and they grant him his life.

Schulz I, 38–40

47 The Huntsman of Soest

The sympathetic reader will have learnt from the previous part how ambitious I had become in Soest, where I sought and found honour, glory and favour in actions for which others would have been punished. Now I will tell how my foolishness misguided me even further so that I lived in continuous danger to body and life. I was so eager to chase after honour and glory that I could hardly sleep and when I fostered such caprices and lay awake many a night to invent new feints and tricks, I had fantastic ideas. So I invented a type of shoe which one could wear back to front so that the heel came under the toes; at my own expense I had 30 different pairs made. When I distributed them among my men and went on a raiding excursion, it was impossible to trace us; because sometimes we wore these and sometimes our ordinary boots, with the others in our kitbags. It appeared, if somebody reached a spot where I ordered a change of shoes that according to our tracks two parties had met, and thereafter had disappeared altogether. If, however, I kept these new shoes on all the time, it looked as if I were approaching a place where I had already been, or as if I had left a place to which I was going! So were my sorties, if they left any tracks, more confusing than a maze, so that those who pursued me by my tracks found it impossible to catch up with me or to bring me into their nets. Often I was quite close to the enemy who searched for me far away, and more often I was some miles away from the copse which they would surround and search in trying to capture me.

In the same way as I arranged it with the patrols on foot, so I tricked the enemy when I was on horseback. For it was not unusual for me to dismount at crossroads and have the horseshoes set back to front. The common advantages that a soldier takes if he is weak on patrol and yet from his footprints appears strong, or if he is strong and would like to be considered weak, all these appeared to me such common tricks, that I think them unworthy of description.

Besides that I invented an instrument with which I could hear at night, if there was no wind, a trumpet blow three hours' walking distance away, a horse's neigh or a dog's bark at two hours' distance, and hear men's talk at one hour's distance. This art I kept very secret and gained much fame

thereby, for it appeared to everyone unimaginable. During the day
however this instrument, which I kept together with a telescope in my
pocket, was of little use except in a lonely, quiet place, for with it I could
hear everything, from horses or cattle to the smallest bird in the air, or the
frog in the water, or whatever in the whole district moved or uttered a
noise. And all this sounded as if I were in the middle of a market among
men and beasts where each makes itself heard and because of the shouting
of one you cannot understand the other. I know very well that up to this
hour there are still people who will not believe what I have just told;
however, whether they believe it or not it is the truth. With such an
instrument I can hear a man's voice at night when he speaks in ordinary
tones, even if he be as far away from me that I could just distinguish his
clothes through a good telescope by daylight. However I blame nobody
for not believing what I am now writing because none of those believed
who saw with their own eyes when I used this instrument and told them: 'I
hear horsemen riding, for the horses are shod! I hear peasants coming for
the horses go unshod! I hear cartmen but they are only peasants for I
recognize their dialect! Musketeers are coming, about so many, as I hear
the clattering of their shoulderbelts! In this or that direction there is a
villlage, for I hear the cocks crowing and the dogs barking! There goes a
herd of cattle for I hear sheep bleating, cows lowing and pigs grunting!'
My comrades in the beginning thought these words were jokes, fooleries
and boasts. Later when indeed they found I always foretold the truth, all
was explained by black magic and that which I had told them was revealed
to me by the devil and his mother. So I assume the sympathetic reader will
think likewise. Nevertheless through all that, I often miraculously and
cleverly escaped the enemy if he by chance had news of me and came to
seize me. I am convinced that if I had revealed my knowledge to someone
it would have come into common use, as it would have been extremely
useful to men in war, especially at sieges. But now back to my story.

If I was not on patrol, I went out looting and neither horses, cows, pigs
nor sheep were safe from me in their stalls, which I stole from miles
around. To avoid being trailed I knew how to put boots or shoes on cattle
and horses until I brought them to a much used highway. Besides I shod
the iron on the horses back to front, or if they were cows and oxen I put
the shoes on them which I had ordered to be made specially and brought
them thus to safety. The huge, fat swine-fellows who in their laziness do
not like to travel by night, I knew how to move on in a masterly way,
however they might grunt and decline. I made a well salted porridge with
meal and water and soaked a sponge therein, to which I had tied a strong
rope and let those that I wanted to keep swallow the sponge full of

porridge, keeping the rope in my hand, whereupon they followed patiently without further dispute, and paid the bill with hams and sausages.

H. J. C. von Grimmelshausen, *Simplicius Simplicissimus*, translated by H. Weissenborn and L. Macdonald (London, 1964), 169–71

48   Small-pox and quack medicines

I thought of the parson in Lippstadt who had counselled me to employ my means and my youth in study. But it was much too late to trim the wings when the bird had flown away. O swift and fatal transformation! Four weeks ago I was a fellow who moved princes to admiration, charmed the ladies, appeared to the people as a masterpiece of nature, indeed an angel, but was now so despicable that the dogs pissed on me. Thousands of ideas raced through my head as to what I should do now that the innkeeper had thrown me out of the house as I could pay him no longer. Gladly I would have enlisted but no recruiting officer would accept me as a soldier for I looked like a scabby cuckoo. I could not work being still too weak and not accustomed to any kind of labour. Nothing consoled me more than that summer was approaching and if needs be I could shelter behind a hedge for no one would allow me to enter a house. I still had my fine clothing which I had ordered for the journey, including my knapsack full of precious linen which no one wanted to buy for fear of getting my disease. So I took the knapsack on my back, my sword in my hand and the road beneath my feet; this led me to a small town which boasted an apothecary. There I went and had an ointment prepared to remove the pock marks from my face, and as I had no money I gave the apprentice a beautiful, soft shirt, he being not so particular as the other fools who would not accept clothes from me. I had hopes that if I could rid myself of these shameful spots, my misery would vanish. The apothecary consoled me that in a week's time little would be seen except the very deep scars which the pocks had eaten into my face, and this gave me some courage. It happened to be market day in the town and there was a tooth-drawer who gained much money by selling quack medicine to the people. 'Fool,' I said to myself, 'Why don't you also start such a trade? Haven't you been long enough with Monseigneur Canard and learnt enough to cheat a credulous peasant and make your living? You must truly be a miserable simpleton!'

Grimmelshausen, 264

49   The good old times in the army, 1631

In a discussion between Captain Schnepfs, Veit Schrammen and Lentze Krumhold, the captain talks of the 'good old times'. From a broadside of 1631.

So let's compare this present war with only those that were fought in Emperor Maximilian II's and Rudolph II's times, and you'll notice a big difference between the combatants of those times and the soldiers of today. In short, you must admit that today's warfare is hardly a shadow of what it was. . . .

Didn't we used to have an impressive and extensive system of law and order in the Roman Empire? Whenever a war against its hereditary and open enemies was undertaken, it had to take place with the advice and according to the will of the Electors and Estates. Thereafter orders were issued to the Circles as to how to assess, collect and audit a general tax for the upkeep of the war. In those times there was none of this about emergency levies, exactions and suchlike coercion. Instead, reputable, brave commanders and officers were appointed who were highly esteemed by cavalrymen and footsoldiers, and quickly attracted good chaps to their musters, who were then led against the enemy. Unless it happened to be a frontier guard, a regiment seldom kept in being for more than a year: by the time winter came it would be disbanded. So the poor old inhabitants were not plagued with winter billeting. Nowadays we hear of nothing but billets, musters, forced taxes and other extortions. And among those responsible for all this are foreign and other undesirable skivers, swindlers – stonemasons and smiths and suchlike – who when they have harvested enough money and property, clear out and leave others the husks, especially whenever a real campaign is in the offing.

> E. von Frauenholz (ed.), *Das Heerwesen in der Zeit des Dreissigjährigen Krieges* I *Das Söldnertum* (Munich, 1938), 6 n

50   An uneasy demobilization of Swedish Allies, 1649

The Swedes' official historian, Samuel Pufendorf, describes the difficulties of demobilization for the Swedish-Allied army of 1649 in his account of the Swedish–German war.

So all native Swedish soldiers were collected during the whole autumn [of 1649] at the sea coast, which amounted to nearly 19,000 cavalry and foot. Likewise a few of the German cavalry regiments were disbanded; the

regiments of foot were reduced, and their spare officers dismissed.
Although the queen [Christina of Sweden's government] wanted to keep
20,000 of the best German footsoldiers in her service, this was not to be.
For the experienced soldiers were tired of war . . . and when they were
forced to stay in service against their will, rebellions broke out in different
places.

Those that were in Schweinfurt [Franconia] not only chased their
officers away but also demanded immediate payment of their monthly
salaries. Yet because of Wrangel's presence, they not only remained loyal
but also handed over those who had started the rebellion, who paid for it
with their heads. The rest once more had to swear allegiance to the queen,
but nevertheless most of them ran away.

As they were being led to the sea coast, those from Neumark
[Brandenburg] refused to march any further as their officers had been
disbanded, instead demanding their own dismissal and pay. A Swedish
regiment encircled them and, after their arms had been taken from them,
lots were to have been cast to select 14 of them for hanging. Yet the
Nürnbergers interceded on their behalf, and they were driven off without
being dismissed or paid.

Frauenholz, 22 n

V   Townsmen, nobles and clergy

51   Brawling townsmen and troops, Wiedenbrück, 1632, 1642

On 20 February 1632 a lieutenant colonel, Timan Theodorus de Lintelo, forced his way into our town with a company of cavalry and three companies of footsoldiers. They were new recruits who had not been made up to full strength. But among the youngsters was a corporal from Tilly's regiments called Scholer who was in the town with one hundred musketeers. They had been billeted here for a year. They took over the New Gate early one morning and unlocked it. The burghers tried to stop them but failed since the soldiers already possessed the keys. For a while they all fought each other, so that two soldiers were left dead and from among the burghers, the stablehand of Hinrich Bierman, as well as many wounded. The burghers had to pay a sum of money to the colonel and finally the troop strength was made up to six companies of foot and one company of horse. They stayed here for 16 weeks and left on 8 July. . . .

On 20 May 1642 the common soldier who was serving under Captain Domstorff was beheaded because he had killed with his sword our fellow burgher, Johan Gronen, who was innocent. May God have mercy on his soul. Amen.

Kothe, 16, 18

52   Execution of a traitor, Wiedenbrück, 1642

Between Saturday and Sunday 8 September [1641] at midnight the commandant from Lippstadt tried for the fifth time to capture this town [Wiedenbrück]. God Almighty mercifully prevented this and instead two prisoners were captured along with a 12-foot long plank.

On 10 September [1641] at midnight the same commandant returned with many troops to make his sixth attempt at taking the town, which again was prevented by the grace of God. He was beaten off and three prisoners were taken along with a portable brushwood bridge. . . .

On 26 May [1642] the traitor, who was born in the parish of Warselo [between Catholic Wiedenbrück and Protestant Lippstadt] and who had

wished to betray this town [Wiedenbrück] in the previous year on the 8
and 10 September to the Hessian commandant in Lippstadt, was
beheaded on the Liebfrauen market place, and then cut into four. Each
quarter was hung on a half-gallows in front of the town gates. The head
was spiked onto the town council judge's post and erected behind the
castle at the place where the traitor had planned to let the enemy soldiers
into the town. May Almighty God be praised that his treacherous intent
was not successful and finally stopped. May the Dear Lord henceforth
protect us from treason and incursions of the enemy. Amen.

Kothe, 17–18

53 Olmütz under the Swedes, 1643

The Moravian town of Olmütz is left to the Swedes, who use its resources for army
recreation, as described in this extract from the diary of the town scribe, Friedrich
Flade.

Imperial War Commissar Colonel Miniati moved out of town with the
Cracowian recruits at about six o'clock on the morning of 15 June. At
noon Major General Wittenberg and Colonel Dörffling came and
demanded in the name of His Excellency, Swedish Fieldmarshal
Torstensson, that the town pay 150,000 ransom.

As the town was unable to pay, we finally reduced this to 30,000 after
negotiating and pleading day and night, by secretly promising 4,000
reichstalers to the commissar and 4,000 to be quit of the remainder.

The fieldmarshal moved on to Silesia on the 16th together with the rest
of the troops, taking the money that had been given and leaving behind as
garrison three regiments, namely Horn's and Hammerstein's horse, and
one of foot commanded by Colonel Königam, who was also installed as
kommandant of the town.

On St John the Baptist's Day, Colonel Königam was ordered to move
on, and Colonel George Paikul took his place, who soon demanded on
top of the agreement 100 reichstalers weekly, which the town councillors
were to provide out of their own pockets.

On 1 July Horn's regiment of horse moved on from here to Silesia after
plundering many of the leading burghers' houses, after which Lieutenant
Colonel Wancke arrived with the life regiment of dragoons. Soldiers and
especially their officers robbed the leading burghers' houses of
noteworthy precious items and took away whatever they could find.

On the 5th on the stern command of the kommandant, Colonel Paikul,
the town council ordered provisions of bread and beer alone amounting
to 48 measures of flour a day to be baked for 1,578 musketeers and

dragoons, as well as 14 barrels of beer a day. On top of this the kommandant desires that the common soldier be given one groschen per day in money for meat.

On the 18th the kommandant ennumerated the following points:

1   That the 4,000 reichstalers which were granted and promised to His Excellency [Torstensson] be paid over without fail here next Wednesday and Thursday.

2   That as from next week each and every soldier be given by the town council and clergy one reichstaler for better provisioning.

3   That each and every stablehand [*Knecht*] be given twice weekly each time half a fluid measure of wine.

Jessen, 392–4

54   Ennoblement lampooned

Simplicissimus becomes an upstart noble.

Yet I did not stop here, but decorated my best horse, which Harum-Scarum had taken from the Hessian captain, with saddle, harness and armour to such an extent that, when I was mounted thereon, people might well have taken me for a second Knight St George. Nothing irked me more than to know I was no nobleman so that I could have dressed my servant and my stablelad in my livery. I thought to myself, all things have their beginning: if you have a coat of arms you have your own livery, and as soon as you become an ensign you must have your own seal though you are not a nobleman.

I had not been pregnant long with such ideas when, through a count Palatine I acquired a coat of arms. This consisted of three red masks in a white field, and as a crest on the helmet, the head and shoulders of a young jester dressed in calfskin with a couple of hare's ears and decorated with little bells. For that I thought would suit my name best as I was called Simplicius. Thus I would make use of the fool to remind me in my future high position continuously of what kind of a fellow I had been in Hanau, in order not to become too arrogant, although I had now already no swinish opinion of myself.

In this way I became truly the first of my name, of my lineage and coat of arms, and if anyone had ridiculed me, doubtlessly I would have challenged him with the sword or a pair of pistols.

Grimmelshausen, 200

55–6   Nobles' tax arrears

55   Lippe, 1624

Count Simon VII threatens to fine and distrain seven nobles if they do not pay arrears of their monthly military occupation tax of one taler per hundred morgen of land (62 acres) within the next eight days.

We Simon, etc., bid our dear, stern and loyal, and herewith named, settled and privileged noble our favour and furthermore wish to add that although of late because of outstanding urgent matters concerning the country [of Lippe] an assembly [*Communicationstag*] was called and held, that all the patriots [*Patrioten*] there assembled out of great urgency were unanimous in agreeing through majority vote that for the duration of this emergency and in order to ease the common burden each settled and privileged noble should contribute and send in without exception from each hundred morgen [i.e. 62 acres] of land that he holds one taler. And we fully expected that each loyal noble would show himself obedient and make effective payment of this grant.

Yet we find not without great displeasure that instead of full and correct payment there has been great delay and negligence against our orders and our usual patience, and also against the present well known emergency, which instead has been treated almost with contempt.

Although we are prepared to leave this matter as it is at present, yet since the emergency is still with us, and since this tax grant is now especially urgently needed for the rescue of the common well-being and also for upholding the fatherland [*dieser bewilligten steur zu dess gemeinen wesens auch erhaltung dass Vatterlandts*], so we order you herewith finally without any further communication that each and everyone pay his quota of assessed monthly back tax within eight days from this date, on pain of 30 gulden fine, to our court chamberlain, Simon Schwartz, without fail, or in case this is missed, on the next following day after this period has run out, to pay the fine on top of the tax arrears or be subject to distraint [*Execution*] without exception. And let everyone be warned and protect himself from damage. That is our earnest intention.

Given in our Castle Detmold, 6 December 1624
            Simon, Count and Noble Lord of Lippe.

There follow names and amounts in arrear. Seven nobles from the families of Donop, Friesenhausen and Mengersen owed between two and ten months arrears each of nobles' emergency land tax.

Staatsarchiv Detmold, L 11 IV 5a

56   Lippe, 1637

Circular letter among the nobility, warning each other to pay their taxes or suffer distraint by military force and accepting no responsibility for any violence attempted against those who fail to pay.

Noble, stern and steadfast, generous, dear cousins, relatives by marriage, and good friends.

We inform you with the enclosed letter what the count and ruling lord, Lord Johan Bernhard of Lippe, has graciously ordered us, as appointed Estates' counsellors [*Landräte*] to send to you.

There is now acute danger as everyone must well know, and as is made quite explicit in the count's letter, that violent distraint for unpaid taxes will take place and that we must take further measures to prevent the country [of Lippe] from ruin, since we would dearly like to see every nobleman spared these unpleasant threats.

We therefore remind you in friendship and loyalty that each and everyone of you pay in full his outstanding tax quotas within the next eight days in good, hard currency from the date of receipt of this demand and according to the enclosed schedule, to the tax-receiver of the nobility, Heinrich von Exter, without exception.

In the undesired case of non-payment, since the armies of *both* sides have been forced by circumstances to threaten us with military distraint for unpaid arrears, those nobles still in arrears will be handed over by our ruling count to make their own arrangements with the armies.

Let everyone be warned of this and find the correct way of protecting himself from damage with the utmost urgency.

Signed with a plea for the protection of God, in Lemgo, 19 September 1637.

> With helpful wishes, sealed and signed by
> Donop, Grote, Rubel, Grote
> the four noble *Landräte*,
> and the signature of 20 noble and exempted
> establishments.
>
> Staatsarchiv Detmold, L 10 Titel 2 Nr 11

57   Nobles' political in-fighting, Lippe, 1635

Nobleman Grote gives an account of Lippe politics and tries to persuade Levin von Donop to return to the county and thus strengthen the opposition within the nobility and territorial assembly.

To *Drost* Levin von Donop on Wöbbel, Donop and Lüderhoff.

Noble and stern, generous benefactor and esteemed friend. That Your Noble Honour has been out of the country [Lippe] for so long has no doubt been due to urgent business, but I have missed your presence terribly.

Concerning our case [on behalf of the Lippe nobility] at [the federal cameral tribunal in] Speier [in dispute with the towns of Lippe over tax assessment] I have written to Master Robbich our lawyer [*Syndicus*] and he can inform Your Noble Honour about it.

Otherwise we have become at our Estates' meetings and territorial assemblies very meek people, promising to pay one thousand after another in taxes. In the process we forget our real interests, and even payment itself. *Res valde suspecta invisa.* It would take too much to explain it all here.

Although the peasant has been plagued with almost unbearable amounts of war tax, it has helped little since we are still in great danger because of the war situation. Our liberties [*liberteth*] are under very serious attack.

And there is hardly anything more urgent than that Your Noble Honour returns home as soon as possible, since there is no one else speaking up for our liberties. Unfortunately there are far too many 'yes-men' [*Placentiner*].

The territorial assembly at Cappel was so rowdy that nothing could be agreed or minuted, other than that we granted away those thousand talers and received very little gratitude.

'De quo plura Sibaeus' spoke to me in Detmold complaining painfully that the weak points in Your Noble Honour's lawsuit were still being dealt with prejudicially. So I hope that Your Honour will come home swiftly to deal with these general and personal matters.

The war from outside is dangerous to us, yet the war within even more so [*Der krig von auseen ist vns geferlich, doch die Jnlendschen simulteten gehen vohr*].

18 November 1635,

Your Noble Honour's obedient servant, Heinrich Grote.

Staatsarchiv Detmold, L 10 Titel 1 Nr. 7

58   A decade in retrospect

Superintendent Andreä looks back to the 1620s not without nostalgia and pride.

[1624] Once the plague of debased coins, through which I also lost about 800 gulden, had ended and prices had returned more or less to normal, despite which the common man suffered from shortage of everything, all roads were full of beggars. Soon even citizens ceased to feel shame and joined them, and so the laziest and most disreputable people demanded bread from strangers. The few who remained were expected to carry this burden and they were in no position to do so.

That is why I thought of a proper way to supply the needs of the poor whereby the lazy were driven out. I finally arranged it so that alms collected from the citizens should feed the children of the poor twice daily at the hospital, that the aged and infirm should receive their alms at home, but that those who were busy at school or in a craft should have their tuition and apprenticeship paid for and be kept at their tasks. Although I tried to go further, the town council refused to accept more good advice and even tried to obstruct the willingness of the citizens to help.

[1626] In this year there was such a price increase that great droves of beggars including whole families were driven by hunger to leave their homelands, wander around and camp outside the houses of the citizens. With much difficulty and effort I organized a public collection of alms from everyone, partly to cater to the needs of the citizens and partly also to provide outsiders with a fair amount of provisions to speed them on their way. Although relief had been so difficult to organize, its success was extraordinary that from this time [1626] until 1631, when it ceased, over one million poor were fed, supported and sent on – a memorable example for posterity, showing what a small number of citizens can achieve when they unite in Christian love and unlock the doors that often seal the resilient hearts of peasants.

[1628] In this year I first made friends with Johann Gerhard, one of the finest theologians of our time. This was one of the best things that ever happened to me. Since this man who was as great in matters theoretical as he was in matters practical [*der in der Theorie so gross war wie in der Praxis*] agreed with my views and my attempts to improve Christianity, so that with the same spirit and desire he strove to improve behaviour among us, and he abhorred the slime of wantonness. How very different from all those to whom every devout sigh seems suspect and who are satisfied with nothing other than that which smells of theological dispute. Just as there is nothing missing in religion, so by contrast church discipline has very many shortcomings, which Gerhard recognized and exposed together with me. This he often discussed with me in confidence through letters which to my great sorrow I have lost. . . .

[1629] In this year many people had to emigrate, and the times were especially harsh for clergymen and church servants who found it difficult to secure asylum. With a tract in three parts I tried to proselyte, and arouse steadfastness and compassion, not without good use since this task produced partly more generosity and partly easier refuge. . . .

This is the end of the decade [1620s] in which I experienced a number of struggles especially to build up my church. Although it cost me much sweat, I did not find it unpleasant but rather spiced with many Christian satisfactions, and I would regard it as the best time of my life.

Andreä, 57–60

59 A Protestant is martyred, Württemberg, 1634

At this point I cannot keep silent about Kaspar Nikolaus who, although a very ordinary, simple man, had much religion in him, being uncommonly ready to serve his superiors by carrying out most conscientiously anything that he was ordered to do. Hence he was allowed to collect alms in the inns, and he also had the task of keeping the boys in order in church. The former office he carried out with pauline zeal, and the latter with the censoriousness of Cato.

When this unfortunate man fell into the claws of the enemy and was asked whether he was one of those Swedish scoundrels, he replied that he was a Christian and could not deny that his thoughts were wholly with the Swedes. Hereupon he was crudely beaten but he was not in the slightest cowed. He confessed that he lived like one who was on the side of the Swedes, and that he was prepared as such to die. At this he was severely cut about the body, receiving wounds that were, however, not fatal. That is why he was then set alight, and when he at last realized that he was dying, he kept to his Christian and Swedish faith with unshakeable courage until his last breath under extensive torture.

He said that he was certain that with the king of Sweden he could expect to reach heaven, and so he died a devout martyr. It is worth that his name shall neither disappear from among the simple confessors of Christ, nor that the three orphans that he leaves behind shall be forgotten.

Andreä, 77–8

60 Exile and short-term refuge, 1634

[During the pillage of Calw by Croat Imperial troops in September 1634] I never totally forsook my flock and only sought to escape from falling into the hands of the enemy. I joined a band of women and children soon amounting to more than 200 people. Like ants we scurried over hills and rocks. The beneficial influence of Heaven helped us continuously throughout this time. If we had bad weather we would have fared even worse than we did.

After it became known that the town [Calw in Württemberg] had been burnt down, we escaped to Aichelberg, a rough place. We had agreed among ourselves where each of us should hide but since our presence had been betrayed to the enemy, we were barely able to escape a quarter of an hour before we would have been totally ruined. At this the enemy became angry and vented his wrath upon the richest peasant in the place, who after hideous torture was burnt along with his house.

After going about 20 miles as if swept on by the wind we arrived in the depth of night at Gernsbach, to the great consternation of the citizens there, who at first thought we were enemies. Their perplexity soon turned to indignation which nearly led to our harm. We heard people shout in the open streets that the dogs from Calw should be clubbed to death. Yet the kindness of others, above all merchant Johann Gross, although he was of different religious faith, ended our fear and atoned for the mistake that had been made about us. It gave us two days of refuge and comfort.

Since the enemy was also active in these parts and pillaging the whole neighbourhood, and since we were nearly encircled, we decided to make an attempt to ask the victor for mercy. But to our further consternation we had to flee once again into the hills where no one could readily follow us. From there we wandered around, divided into smaller bands, and on the 15 September alone with my nephew John Joshua and son Gottlieb I hid in the deep Lauterbach valley near the stream in a barn on the fields. We spent the night calmly and also the next one.

Since our lodging was moved to another barn where a certain Peter Schill, whom I must praise for his great honesty among the wood-folk, provided us with food and drink, our lack of caution led us back to Gernsbach where we scarcely avoided falling into the net of the enemy. As we lived scattered about all the secret places in Obertsrot, Hilpertsau, Reichtal, Weissenbach, Langenbrand and elsewhere, the hue and cry was raised after us and huntsmen were hired who knew the forests to track us down with their dogs. We saw them in the distance and became heartily dispirited, but also took a serious warning from the event.

I finally arrived at a peasant's place where the wife was nearing her childbirth, and I had a sleepless night since three hours before dawn I had climbed over the peaks of the hills, gone through hill and dale and eventually arrived back at my own vineyard where I had placed my little son Ehrenreich [aged ten], and in which farm we now spent our exile [*exilierte*]. I found my little son much weakened and unable to stand cold and hunger. The Lord took him and released his spirit into the freedom

of Heaven on the 20 September. But shortly before this I had already left.
We were called back in a letter from our friends, since everything, as far as
the times allowed, was back in order, which accorded with the enemy's
own best interest.

When I saw my beloved town of Calw in ashes and rubble – it was
however not the first time that I had seen a town in ruins – I felt a cold
shudder and I brooded repeatedly on that which I neither can nor wish to
repeat now. What struck me most deeply was that long ago I had already
prophesied the calamity, and that my prophecy had now come true in as
much as it had also included me.

Andreä, 80–83

VI Military commanders

61   Mansfeld in defeat, 1621

After the Battle of the White Mountain, Mansfeld held on in Bohemia with his army of ten to twenty thousand, trying to exact payment of two million gulden and to negotiate peace. By early 1621 he was further threatened by Electoral Saxony reporting his moves to the League under Tilly's Bavarians. In this document Mansfeld appeals to the Elector of Saxony to protect him and intercede for him with the Emperor and the Bohemian Estates in his need to continue bartering for the control of key towns in Bohemia in order to pay for his army and to defend the Palatinate. In return, Mansfeld offers not only to leave the Saxon army alone, but also to surrender his towns to Saxon troops, as well as to pledge his own self to the Saxon Elector.

Mansfeld failed. Saxony remained hostile, and the Saxon army continued to report Mansfeld's movements to Tilly and the soldiers of the Emperor and of the Catholic League.

Ernest, Count of Mansfeld to John George, Elector of Saxony, Türschenreut, 19 April 1621.

I have not avoided submissively informing Your Electoral Grace that my ready and standing army is not intended to do any damage or to molest Your Electoral Grace's locally stationed garrisons, but rather to protect the Electoral Palatinate from enemy invasion. And also, because the town of Pilsen, which I have up to now held as security for my large financial claims from the crown of Bohemia, has treasonably been bought through Colonel Frenken and partly through my captains, as also to maintain for my further security Ellenbogen, Tabor, Wittingau and other places, I entertain the submissive hope that Your Electoral Grace, as a most understanding, German-minded [*Teutschgesinnter*] and most praiseworthy ruler, will stay graciously inclined towards me, a poor chevalier who lays every store by equitably remaining in your favour.

Besides which I submissively bid you to move towards arbitrating matters in order that His Imperial Majesty's army give up the siege of above-mentioned Ellenbogen, and leave me unmolested with my securities until my soldiers have received their fair pay.

Further I beg Your Electoral Grace not only to take these above mentioned places with their privileges and freedoms under your gracious protection but also, in order that I and my soldiers shall receive our just payment, graciously to intercede for us with His Roman Imperial Majesty in order that the Bohemian Estates carry this out in all seriousness.

In return I herewith assure Your Electoral Grace not to engage in hostilities against your army. And to show you my good faith, I am at your command to evacuate to you Ellenbogen and the other places, provided this genuinely helps me to obtain a fair recompense from the crown of Bohemia, which demand runs to a great sum [two million gulden].

With this in mind I have also written to Your Electoral Grace's General-Oberst-Wachtmeister at Eger, and hope meanwhile that he establishes good relations and will cease all hostile activities, in return for which I will also issue suitable orders to my own soldiers.

As I now hold, honour and respect Your Electoral Grace as my gracious Elector and Lord, also as highest patron, let Your Electoral Grace also give me your gracious confidence that the same be for the submissive well-being of all, wherefore I recognize myself as willing and obliged with my modest service to wait upon you.

submissively etc.

Ernest, Count of Mansfeld.

L. Ütterodt zu Scharffenberg, *Ernst Graf zu Mansfeld* (Gotha, 1867), 742–3

62–5   Wallenstein

62   Wallenstein's contract with Emperor Ferdinand II, Göllersdorf, 1632

An account in the newsbook, *Theatrum Europaeum*.

The following are the conditions which were agreed when appointment to the generalship was made:

1   That the duke of Friedland be not only His Roman Imperial Majesty's, but also the whole Austrian house's and the crown of Spain's generalissimo.

2   That the generalship be conferred upon him in *absolutissima forma*.

3   That His Imperial Majesty should not appear in person with the army and even less should he have personal command over it, instead when the kingdom of Bohemia recovers and is conquered again, the king should reside in Prague and Don Balthasar shall supply 12,000 men to protect Bohemia to remain there until a universal peace has stabilized the Holy

Roman Empire. For he, the duke of Friedland, finds that the Bohemians must have a real ruler with the personal presence of their king in their own country. In this way the Emperor and his general will be protected all the more from rebellion.

4   He should have as security an Imperial pledge on an Austrian hereditary territory as recompense for his regular expenses.

5   As recompense for his extraordinary expenses, he should be allowed to exercise the highest jurisdiction in the Empire over the territories that he occupies.

6   The right to confiscate lands in the Empire shall be his *in absolutissima forma*, in such a way that neither the *Reichshofrat* nor the treasury nor the *Reichskammergericht* at Speyer [Imperial federal courts] shall pretend to have any power in the matter, be it in cases of general or particular import.

7   As in confiscation of lands so also in granting pardons, he, the duke of Friedland, shall be allowed to act as he pleases. If anyone should obtain a safe conduct and pardon from the Imperial court, such shall have no validity unless it is especially endorsed by the duke of Friedland, and it shall apply in good faith and by word of mouth and not in full substance.

8   A genuine pardon is to be only sought from, and granted by, the duke of Friedland. For in this matter the Emperor would be too lenient and allow it to occur that anyone could be pardoned at the Imperial court, and in this way the means with which to remunerate colonels and officers, as well as looking after the mercenaries as is fit, would be cut off.

9   As it is inevitable that some time or other negotiations for peace will be started in the Empire, so let it be that the duke of Friedland's private interests among other things concerning the duchy of Mecklenburg shall also be included in any agreements.

Schulz I, 124–6

63   Wallenstein's last illness, 1633–4

Wallenstein's apothecary at Pilsen produced an account covering the relatively brief period from 25 December 1633 to 20 February 1634. It is full of an amazing number of items but not as revealing as one might wish, since it lists often only very vague items like powder, plaster, concoction, juice or drink without closer definition. One should also remember that after Wallenstein's murder his personal apothecary, Zacharias Venediger, sent in a much higher bill for 700 fl, as against 139 fl for this one from the apothecary at Pilsen. Yet if one analyses the latter account more closely, one finds that severe constipation was the basic problem. . . . Heartburn

[pyrosis] must have affected him very frequently, especially at night. . . .
One may assume that he suffered from an illness of the stomach and
intestine. . . . He also took organic therapy with preparations from
heart, lung, liver, spleen and kidney of calves, lambs or pigs, called
Beuschel, and often taken in wine. . . .

The general term, *Beuschel*, gives no precise indication of what specific
animal organs were used at which exact point of medical treatment. For
example, pancreas preparations were used when this gland near the
stomach discharging digestive secretion into the duodenum was
malfunctioning. . . .

Liver preparations were used in haemorrhages, gout, cirrhosis of the
liver and gall-stones.

Kidney preparations were used against nephritis and urine poisoning
or *Urämie*. If one could be certain that these medicines, mentioned under
the term *Beuschel* in the apothecary's account, were kidney preparations,
then one could accept the new hypothesis mentioned by L. Kroeber-
Keneth in his *Buch der Graphologie* on page 225, that Wallenstein was
suffering in the last months of his life from *Urämie* which caused him to
have hallucinations or delusions [*Bewusstseinsbetrübungen*]. The added
prescription of medicines to ease urination which can be found in this
apothecary's account further strengthens the likelihood of that
hypothesis. Unfortunately we cannot know for certain.

> G. Mann, *Wallenstein* (Frankfurt-am-Main,
> 1971), 1180–82

64–5   The death of Wallenstein, 1634

The assassination of Wallenstein in the Bohemian town of Eger on 25 February
1634 was enigmatic to say the least. Immediately, the event became newsworthy.
Early accounts (like the first one outlined here) made the most of it. Later
historians' accounts (like the second one here) were more palatable. Yet a sense of
tragic drama remains.

64   A contemporary account of the murder of Wallenstein, 1634

The account here apparently appeared a few days after the event, and it seems to
have been published from Dresden. It judges the assassination with a Lutheran
bias and gives the following details.

Emperor Ferdinand II secretly ordered his arrest, and shortly before
Wallenstein could unite with the Swedes under Duke Bernhard of
Weimar, he was murdered with his closest followers at Eger on 25
February 1634.

Wallenstein is sitting in bed and hearing a noise he goes towards the door, whereupon Colonel Butler appears and pushes a jagged pike [*Partisan*], which Butler holds in his hands, into Wallenstein's body. Notwithstanding this, Wallenstein tries to get to his sword, but is prevented and hewn down by Butler with a third blow. A fourth blow is given when Wallenstein is already stretched out, and as his guts spill out Butler says: 'Ugh, the rebellious scoundrel has been taking too much tobacco today: that's why he stinks so.' [*Pfuy der rebellische Schelm hatt heute Taback gesoffen, davon stincket er also.*]

> Niedersächsisches Staatsarchiv, Hannover,
> Cal. Br. 11, 6 Nr. 198

65   A historian's account

Wallenstein had just taken a bath and was just about to go to get some sleep. His cup-bearer, who had brought him his sleeping draught in a golden bowl, met the intruders and wanted to advise them not to disturb the master's rest. But they struck and wounded the cup-bearer, and raised the cry of 'rebels'. While Wallenstein, upon hearing this commotion, began to move, clothed as he was only in a shirt, towards the window, presumably to call the guard, Captain Devereux with his accomplices burst open the door and screamed these words at Wallenstein: 'Scoundrel and traitor' [*Schelm und Verrater*]. Did Wallenstein have any idea of what was going on? Did he feel that his last move of outrage which he had just made was now immediately calling the revenge of the pro-Imperialists down upon his own head? Yes, it seems quite likely that the sequence of events suddenly became clear in his mind. Leaning on a table, moving his lips but not uttering a sound, he spread his arms wide and pushed his chest towards the halberd with which Devereux just stabbed him. The corpse was wrapped in a red cloth and brought into the castle to join the other corpses.

> L. von Ranke, 'Geschichte Wallensteins',
> *Meisterwerke* IX (Munich and Leipzig, 1915),
> 481

VII   Rulers and diplomats

66   Frederick of the Palatinate in defeat, 1621

A picture in the fly-sheet shows Elector Frederick of the Palatinate clinging to the wheel of fortune. At the top he sits in majesty; as the wheel continues to turn, he is thrown off into the sea, from where Dutch fishermen rescue him with their nets.

'Crowns' or *Cronen* (7 lines from the end) has a double meaning – in the sense of the dignity of royalty and in the sense of coins, money.

The former Palatine's fortune and misfortune

> Whosoever wishes to understand fortune and misfortune,
> Let him observe this play of the Palatine.
> Very happy was he in the Empire,
> His like was not easily to be found.
> He lacked neither people nor lands,
> Ruled *wisely* and with *judgement*.
> A wife of royal lineage,
> Who multiplied his high name,
> Was bringing happiness with young heirs.
> His line would not soon die out.
> By rich and poor, by young and old,
> He was held in high esteem,
> Which then was but just,
> For he held the most important Electorate
> Of the four lay Electors:
> He was a jewel of the Holy Roman Empire.
> In sum, he had everything,
> If only he had been satisfied.
> O ambition, you cursed passion:
> Here one can see your poisonous fruit!
> You make glory and honour sweet to many a man
> Until he gets trampled under foot.
> How charming, indeed how elegant,
> How brave and ever fortunate
> Was Palatine Frederick formerly,
> Before pride raised him high.
> The best masters in his council

Here did him the greatest harm.
Plessen, Camerarius
Were not vexed by any toil or trouble,
Until they had raised him to the top
And made him a king.
But that could not last for long
Because he made to use a stranger's country,
His kingdom was not of this world,
Thus he soon fell to the ground.
So where did he fall? Into the deep sea,
Deserted by his whole army.
The United Provinces have drawn him in,
To make a show of their new catch
Whom they display as a showpiece.
Fortune has completely forgotten him,
Has made of him a laughing-stock before the world,
And used him as a mirror,
So that everyone henceforth
Should be satisfied with his own.
How gladly would not his counsellors
Who turned the wheel of fortune too violently
Have again swung him up on high:
But all goes wrong with him,
He has sunk too deep.
Indeed he may well have drowned
Had not Holland helped.
But he is still in a sad plight,
For as he crept out of the net
They promised him nothing more
Than that he might live with them,
Now many good crowns have been squandered.
Formerly he had many folk and lands,
Now he has an empty hand.
Formerly he had a crown on his head,
Now he scarcely has a whole shirt to wear.
    God help poor Frederick
    For he will never get out of this himself.
Printed in the year 1621 [anonymous].

British   Library,   Print   Room,   Foreign
History, 1621, translation adapted from E. A.
Beller, *Caricatures of the Winter King* (Oxford,
1928), plate XIV and 42–3

67   Christian IV in defeat, 1626

In August 1626 Tilly defeated King Christian IV of Denmark at Lutter am
Baremberg in the Lower Saxon Circle. Tilly wrote patronizingly of his royal
adversary in a dispatch to Infanta Isabella in Brussels.

The king of Denmark is clearly a most talented general, as I have seen
myself at Lutter am Bärenberg. Some people will have it that the cause of
his disaster was that he yielded to pressure, others again say that his
understanding has suffered from his fall into Hameln town ditch last year.

He has, however, shown no lack either of courage or of intelligence,
but drew up a plan of the operations for the day in a way which shows his
thorough military skill.

In her reply to Tilly from Brussels, 9 September 1626, Infanta Isabella outlined
the Baltic naval plan, the threat of which eventually played a part in bringing the
Swedes into the war.

The duke of Friedland [Wallenstein] is in pursuit of Mansfeld and
Weimar. We have written to him that if God grants him the success which
we may hope for from his hand, we think it very necessary that he should
at once secure some harbour on the Pomeranian coast in order to prevent
Germany from being invaded from that side by the Swedes or other
enemies.

H. G. R. Reade, *Sidelights on the Thirty Years
War* II (London, 1924), 589–90

68–9   The Emperor Ferdinand II

68   The Edict of Restitution is circumvented in Lippe, 1629

In August 1629, the (Calvinist) government of the county of Lippe in northwest
Germany decided to pay lip-service to the Edict of Restitution in order to forestall
distraint by Imperialist troops as had recently been threatened in the neighbouring county of Schaumburg.

Letter of Hofrichter v. Schwartz to Landdrost v.d. Borch.

I have received certain information from Minden that the Emperor's
commissar, Hein, has arrived in person in Minden, and is especially
ordered to deal with the county of Lippe: namely to repossess the
ecclesiastical lands and properties sequestered after the Passau agreement
[1552], and to reconvert people in the county of Lippe to Roman
Catholicism or to the Augsburg Confession and law, which latter, thank
God, we now also have the choice of – note well, all according to the
choice and decision of the Detmold government.

This commissar was in County Schaumburg the last week, and he

demanded the restitution of all the ecclesiastical lands and properties of
the university there [a Calvinist foundation from 1619]. The Schaumburg
councillors raised considerable objections upon which the commissar
soon went to His Excellency, Tilly. Thus one fears he will ask for military
reprisals.

The Emperor's edict is ordered to be carried out in County
Schaumburg. I suggest that one do likewise here in Lippe. If the
commissar should come and not find that this has been done it is to be
expected that the same will happen here.

Staatsarchiv Detmold, L 41a IV 207

69   The despotism of Ferdinand II is threatened, 1631

A decree of the Emperor, denouncing the armaments pact of the Protestant
territories who were assembled in Leipzig, April 1631. Ferdinand prohibits the
taking of military service under any of the Protestant rulers, forbidding the
payment of all taxes for military purposes to any Protestant rulers as 'against our
will and contrary to the constitutions of the Empire'. He demands the public
display of this Imperial decree and admonishes all territorial rulers and their
subjects to obey him.

Ferdinand etc. . . . To all etc. . . .
We hereby do signify, whereas by letters dated 4 April last the Elector and
duke of Saxen hath given us notice of a conclusion made by the Electors,
States; counsellors, ambassadors, deputies and commissioners (of such
Protestants as were absent), lately assembled at Leipzig, the strangeness
whereof hath much moved and filled with displeasure our Imperial heart,
since that the said Electors, Princes and States have agreed and bound
themselves, quite contrary to our admonitions sent before to the said
Elector of Saxen, *under pretext of an order of execution of the Circles*, to make a
dangerous preparation of war; and, without any signification of their
number and designs, make new already (as from divers parts we are
advertised) *in several Circles, and particularly in our Imperial cities* great levies:

And whereas it is easy to presume, that at this perilous constitution of
the Empire, where the king of Sweden is entered as an enemy and having
already taken whole Pomerania, a part of the Mark of Brandenburg, and
some places [in] Mecklenburg, will daily proceed, and *incite other foreign
forces* to do much:

Where the rebellious town of Magdenburg is not yet brought to
obedience, and where many old dangers do yet appear; such a dangerous
beginning and intent would tend to hinder (and as it were bereave us of)
all means to maintain the wars, now so requisite for the defence and

necessity of the Holy Empire and States thereof; it would further and advantage the power of the enemies; cause yet a greater confusion, troubles and evils, and withal a far greater mistrust and hatred among this nation: Yea (unless it be with all speed withstood) it would bring into the whole Roman Empire of the German Nation (our dear country) a new unquenchable fire whereby the same (which these 800 years hath most sweetly flourished) would now at once be consumed to ashes and wholly overthrown.

Therefore we knowing that our duty requires, that, as Roman Emperor we do prevent all such threatening evils, and that *such agreements and unions are not to be made nor suffered without the knowledge, consent and pleasure of the Roman Emperor*, who we are, but that they are quite contrary unto the laws, orders and constitutions of the Empire, and the dehortations and admonitions made by us being prohibited under great and grievous punishments so that we intend by no means to suffer [allow] the same.

We do hereby admonish, will and command you that you do not give nor permit any place of rendezvous unto troops or soldiers, that are, may or might be levied on the behalf of the said agreement and conclusion made at Leipzig; neither grant any of them passage or pass whatsoever, but rather kill them, as you will answer the contrary at your perils of the punishments expressed in the constitutions of the Empire. . . .

Given, Vienna, 14 May 1631

> *The Continuation of Our Weekly Newes from Forraine Parts*, no. 31 (London, 25 June 1631), Cambridge University Library, Syn. 7.63.327, 7–8

70   Lützen and the death of Gustavus Adolphus, 1632

The Battle of Lützen was fought on 16 November 1632. The first report was circulating the next day. The day after this, 18 November, the account translated here was issued by the Imperialists. By 22 November a printed account of the battle was selling in the streets of Prague.

Report from Dux, 18 November 1632.

The day before yesterday a great battle occurred between His Grace, the Duke of Mecklenburg [Wallenstein] and the King from Sweden on those ramparts where a year ago the confrontation near Leipzig took place. The battle ran from ten o'clock in the morning until well into the dark night. On both sides well up to 15,000 men remained lying on the field, the King is also dead. Herr Feldmarschalk-Leuthenant Holcka has obtained his signet ring and spurs, a musketeer furthermore has his sword. On our side many officers were injured. Herr Graf von Happenheim died in the first onslaught. The enemy took five or six of our standards, but we took about 30 of theirs. So the enemy lost much more than we did and has retired towards Naumburg, while His Grace [Wallenstein] has moved on Leipzig. Further details to follow.

G. Droysen (ed.), *Gedruckte Relationen über die Schlacht bei Lützen* (second edition, Halle, 1903), 4

71   A journey through war-torn Germany, 1636

Extracts from the diary of William Crowne, Gent., a member of the earl of Arundel's embassy to Emperor Ferdinand II, 1636.

From Cologne to Frankfurt all the towns, villages and castles are battered, pillaged and burnt and at every one of our halts we remained on board, every man taking his turn on guard duty.

After passing through a wood, we came to a little village called Neunkirchen along the Main, before reaching Würzburg, early May 1636, which we found quite uninhabited yet with one house on fire. Here, since it was now late, we were obliged to stay all night, for the nearest town was four miles away; but we spent all night walking up and down with carbines in our hands, and listening fearfully to the sounds of shots in the woods around us. We did, however, make use of some of the burning fragments of the house that was on fire, for we used them to roast the meat that was prepared for His Excellency's [the earl of Arundel] supper.

Early next morning, His Excellency went to inspect the church and found that it had been plundered and that the pictures and altar had been desecrated. In the churchyard we saw a dead body, scraped out of the grave, while outside the churchyard we found another dead body. Moreover, we entered many houses but found that all were empty. We hurried on from this unhappy place and learnt later that the villagers had fled on account of the plague and had set that particular house on fire in order to prevent travellers from catching the infection.

Early next morning we continued our journey, passing through Neustadt an der Aisch, which must have been a fine city, though now it lies pillaged and with many houses burnt to the ground. Here, seeing wretched children sitting at their doors almost dying of hunger, His Excellency ordered that food and money should be given to their parents. Next we came to Emskirchen, a miserable village, where we dined on food of our own for there was no food to be had there; and after dinner we passed a succession of pillaged and devastated villages and so entered the region around Nuremberg, passing through the places where the king of Sweden's forces were encamped when the king of Bohemia and my Lord Craven were with him. The Emperor's army had lain entrenched by a large wood in full view of this place, and here it was that the king of Sweden strung up alive, on poles, three of his soldiers who had killed two Swedish commanders and had then traitorously joined the enemy. In the ensuing battle, all three were captured and later executed by their former comrades.

On 8 June [1636] the Emperor [Ferdinand II] granted His Excellency another private audience while, at an audience which he had with the Empress on 10 June, we were permitted the honour of being admitted to kiss her hand. On this same day, seven rebels, the leaders of an armed insurrection of 400 ignorant peasants against the Emperor, were beheaded. The ringleader of the revolt, a fellow who had persuaded himself that no bullet had power to harm him, was led on to the scaffold with his face covered and with two men holding him firmly against the block. Here the executioners seized him firmly by the chest with a massive pair of red-hot pincers and, nailing his right hand to the block, chopped it off. Then, quickly drawing the sword he wore at his side, he cut off the wretched fellow's head which an assistant raised, shouting into the ears of the dead man: 'Jesus, Jesus'. At this juncture, the Jesuit, who had accompanied the criminal and who had been admonishing him for his sins, asked those present to join in prayer for the soul of the dead man. Following this came the man's accomplices, including a young boy, all of whom bore crucifixes in their hands and made their individual confessions at the foot of the scaffold to priests, kissing their hands and feet at the end of every prayer. After these wretches had been beheaded and quartered, two of their confederates were taken on foot about a mile to a place where the body of a priest of theirs, arrested the previous year in the church of Ering, hung on a pole.

On Sunday 12 June, after hearing Mass in their own church, the Emperor with the Empress and the Archduchess dined at the Jesuit College and afterwards watched a play presented to them by the Jesuits and some young students. On 15 June, His Excellency was sumptuously entertained at dinner. . . .

On Sunday 17 July [1636] we left [Rötz in the Upper Palatinate] early, passing through extensive woods where we were in danger of attack from Crabats [Croats] who roam these parts, and accidentally taken completely off our route by an ignorant guide, until we reached the pleasantly situated but entirely ruined town of Bruck in the Upper Palatinate. Here, not more than four families remained of what formerly had been a prosperous place and, when we had gone a little way beyond the town, we saw by the wayside a gallows and scaffold where the Lutheran burghers of Bruck had been hanged – indeed we passed some of the bodies still hanging there. From Bruck we journeyed to Nittenau for dinner, continuing after that to Regensburg through very pleasing scenery and entering the city by crossing rafters laid over the River Regen to take the place of the bridge which had been demolished by gunfire.

F. C. Springell (ed.), *Connoisseur and Diplomat: the Earl of Arundel's Embassy to Germany in 1636* (London, 1963), 59–76

Select bibliography

1 *General works*

J.V. Polišenský, *The Thirty Years War*, translated by R. Evans (London, 1971), is the best analysis despite its heavy reliance on Bohemian and Moravian materials. C. V. Wedgwood, *The Thirty Years War* (London, 1938), is straight narrative, useful for checking dates and facts. G. Pagès, *The Thirty Years War*, translation of the 1939 French original (London, 1971), places the hostilities of the era in the wider context of European diplomacy and politics. T. K. Rabb (ed.), *The Thirty Years War* (Boston, 1964), is useful historiography, reprinting Steinberg's interpretative essay from 1947 and, from older important studies, brief extracts especially from the work of Pekař, Roberts and Tapié. R. R. Ergang, *The Myth of the All-destructive Fury of the Thirty Years War* (Pocono Pines, 1956), is brief polemic, going well beyond Steinberg in playing down the effects of the various campaigns on the German territories. G. Freytag, *Pictures of German Life*, translated by Georgiana Malcolm, II (London, 1862), uses carefully selected horror stories, above all from contemporary chronicles, to present an exaggerated view of overall death and destruction. It is against work like this that Steinberg reacted. H. Kamen and M. Hughes, 'The Thirty Years War', in *European History, 1500–1700* (Sussex Books, 1976), is a short discussion for student use. S. H. Steinberg, *The 'Thirty Years War' and the Conflict for European Hegemony, 1600–60* (London, 1966), is still the best brief introduction to the period. H. U. Rudolf (ed.), *Der Dreissigjährige Kreig. Perspektiven und Strukturen* (Darmstadt, 1977), reprints 17 essays and includes a useful bibliography. L. Bäte (ed.), *Der Friede in Osnabrück 1648* (Oldenburg, 1948), is a very useful commemorative volume. A. W. Ward *et al., The Cambridge Modern History of Europe* IV (1906), contains excellent bibliographies of contemporary printed materials, above all those now in the Acton Collection in Cambridge University Library. Friedrich Schiller, *The History of the Thirty Years War*, translated by A. Morrison (London, 1901), is classic imaginative history written before the rise of archive positivism. T. K. Rabb, *The Struggle for*

Stability in Early Modern Europe (New York, 1975), chapter 11, makes a case for a 'crisis mentality of war horrors', turning especially to the pictorial evidence of Rubens and Callot (pp. 124–45). J. V. Polišenský, *War and Society in Europe 1618–48* (Cambridge, 1978).

2 Political thought

F. Meinecke, *Machiavellism* (London, 1958), looks at the development of *Staatsraison*, and is useful to compare with the Thirty Years War notion of *Kriegsraison*. F. S. Carney (ed. and trans.), *The Politics of Johannes Althusius*, (London, 1964), combines Aristotle with Calvinism; this was a basic influence in the Netherlands and Protestant Germany during the first half of the seventeenth century.

3 Economic and social aspects

H. Kamen, 'The Economic Consequences of the Thirty Years War', *Past and Present* no. 39 (1968), is the best short survey in English. G. Franz, *Der Dreissigjährige Krieg und das Deutsche Volk* (3rd edn, Stuttgart, 1961), still the only demographical survey, has to be used with caution since the author tends to accept the results of local researchers, who are often heavily influenced by the 'death and destruction' school of later nineteenth-century German historiography, and who have often applied archive evidence indiscriminately. G. Benecke, 'The Problem of Death and Destruction in Germany during the Thirty Years War. New Evidence from the Middle Weser Front', *European Studies Review* (July 1972), tries to show how equivocal sources can be. H. Kellenbenz, *The Rise of the European Economy*, revised edn by G. Benecke (London, 1976), is a factual survey. R. Ludloff, 'Industrial Development in Sixteenth- and Seventeenth-Century Germany', *Past and Present* no. 12 (1957). R. Endres, 'Zur wirtschaftlichen und sozialen Lage in Franken vor dem Dreissigjährigen Krieg', *Jahrbuch für fränkische Landesforschung* XXVIII (1968), is the best brief survey of prices, wages and living conditions in Germany up to the Thirty Years War, with especial reference to the excellent literature from Nuremberg. I. Bog, *Die bäuerliche Wirtschaft im Zeitalter des dreissigjährigen Kriegs* (Coburg, 1952), is a classic study of administration in a Franconian rural district. F. Schröer, *Das Havelland im Dreissigjährigen Krieg* (Cologne, 1966), is an excellent local study of a part of Brandenburg. A. E. Christensen, *Dutch Trade to the Baltic about 1600* (Copenhagen, 1941). P. Jeannin, 'Les comptes du Sund', *Revue Historique* (1964). V. Barbour, *Capitalism in Amsterdam in the Seventeenth Century* (Ann Arbor, 1963). J. F. Jameson, 'Willem Usselinx, Founder of the Dutch and Swedish West India

Companies', *Papers of the American Historical Association* (1887). F. J. Bowman, 'Dutch Diplomacy and the Baltic Grain Trade, 1600–60', *Pacific Historical Review* V (1936). A. Öberg, 'Russia and the World Market in the Seventeenth Century', *Scandinavian Economic History Review* III (1955). P. W. Klein, 'The Tripp Family in the Seventeenth Century', *Acta Historiae Neerlandica* I (1966). J. Vlachovič, 'Slovak Copper Boom (to the 1620s)', *Studia Historica Slovaca* I (1963). A. Klimá, 'Industrial Development in Bohemia after the Thirty Years War', *Past and Present* no. 11 (1957). J. S. Kepler, 'Fiscal Aspects of the English Carrying Trade during the Thirty Years War', *Economic History Review* (1972). A. V. Judges, 'Philip Burlamachi: a Financier of the Thirty Years War', *Economica* VI (1926). G. Schöttle, 'Die grosse deutsche Geldkrise von 1620–3, und ihr Verlauf in Oberschwaben', *Württemberger Vierteljahrschrift* XXX (1921). W. A. Shaw, 'Monetary movements of 1600–21 in Holland and Germany', *Transactions of the Royal Historical Society* (1895). M. Reissmann, *Die hamburgische Kaufmannschaft des 17. Jahrhunderts in sozialgeschichtlicher Sicht* (Hamburg, 1975), is a useful study of Hamburg's elites, especially in the prosperous 1630s and 1640s for this important entrepôt. E. Woelkens, *Pest und Ruhr im 16. und 17. Jahrhundert* (Uelzen, 1954), is a classic study of the medical history of an early modern town in Lower Saxony. V. von Klarwill (ed.), *The Fugger Newsletters* (London, 1924), provides useful contemporary background. G. Lammert, *Geschichte der Seuchen, Hungers -und Kriegsnoth zur Zeit des Dreissigjährigen Krieges* (1890, reprinted Wiesbaden, 1971), covers the years 1600–1650 chronologically, listing effects of weather, prices, diseases and war damage. T. K. Rabb, 'The Economic Effects of the Thirty Years War', *Journal of Modern History* XXXIV (1962).

4 Collections of documents

J. Polišenský *et al.*, *Documenta Bohemica Bellum Tricennale Illustrantia* (Prague, 1971–), is a collection of Czech archive materials. K. Müller (ed.), *Die westfälischen Friedensverträge* (Bern, 1966), is the standard edition for student use, in Latin and German. *Acta Pacis Westphalicae* (Münster, 1962–), is the chief source for the peace negotiations of the 1640s. *Briefe und Akten zur Geschichte des dreissigjährigen Krieges* (11 vols, Munich, 1870–1909, new series, 1907–), documents the politics of the Union and the League up to the events of 1618, and also concentrates on the activities of Maximilian of Bavaria. M. Roberts (ed.), *Sweden as a Great Power, 1611–97* (London, 1968).

5   Military systems

E. von Frauenholz, *Das Heerwesen in der Zeit des dreissigjährigen Krieges* (Munich, 1938ff.), is the standard work of reference with many documents. F. Redlich, *De Praeda Militari. Looting and Booty* (Wiesbaden, 1956), is a short background study in English. F. Redlich, *The German Military Enterpriser* (2 vols, Wiesbaden 1964–5), amasses a great amount of detail. F. Redlich, 'Military Entrepreneurship and the Credit System', *Kyklos* X (1957). F. Redlich, 'Contributions in the Thirty Years War', *Economic History Review*, second series XII (1959–60). B. H. Nickle, *The Military Reforms of Prince Maurice of Orange*, Delaware University thesis (1975). G. Parker, *The Army of Flanders and the Spanish Road* (Cambridge, 1972); nothing as masterful as this work is as yet available on central European military systems, despite the mass of work on Wallenstein. M. Ritter, 'Das Kontributionssystem Wallensteins', *Historische Zeitschrift* LIV (1903), is crucial for understanding the system of wartime taxation. F. Redlich, 'Der Marketender', *Vierteljahrschrift für Sozial- und Wirtschaftsgeschichte* XLI (1954), looks at the economic and welfare system in camp. A. Egler, *Die Spanier in der Linksrheinischen Pfalz, 1620–32   Invasion, Verwaltung, Recatholisierung* (Mainz, 1971).

6   Diplomacy and politics

S. R. Gardiner, *Letters etc . . . Relations England–Germany, June 1618 to August 1619* (Camden Society, 1865); with continuation, *August 1619 to March 1620* (Camden Society, 1868); *Mission of Roe to Gustavus Adolphus, 1629–30* (Camden Society, 1875); these are essential documents, especially for the enigmatic policies of James I. F. C. Springell (ed.), *Connoisseur and Diplomat: The Earl of Arundel's Embassy to Germany in 1636 as Recounted in William Crowne's Diary etc.* (London, 1963), is expressive travelogue up the Rhine and across to Austria in a particularly serious war year. M. J. Brown, *Itinerant Ambassador: the Life of Sir Thomas Roe* (Kentucky, 1970). R. B. Mowat, 'The Mission of Sir Thomas Roe to Vienna, 1641–2', *English Historical Review* XXV (1910). J. I. Israel, 'A Conflict of Empires: Spain and the Netherlands, 1618–48', *Past and Present* no. 76 (1977). J. Polišenský, 'Denmark–Norway and the Bohemian Cause', *Festgabe für L. L. Hammerich* (Copenhagen, 1962). J. Polišenský, 'Gallants to Bohemia', *Slavonic and East European Review* XXV (1946–7). E. A. Beller, 'The Mission of Sir Thomas Roe to the Conference at Hamburg, 1638–40', *English Historical Review* XLI (1926). E. A. Beller, 'The Negotiations of Sir Stephen Le

Sieur', *English Historical Review* XL (1925). A. McCabe, 'England's Foreign Policy in 1619', *Mitteilungen des Instituts für Österreichische Geschichte* LVIII (1950). E. Weiss, *Die Unterstützung Friedrichs V von der Pfalz durch Jacob I von England im dreissigjährigen Krieg* (Stuttgart, 1966). I. Hoffmann, *Deutschland im Zeitalter des dreissigjährigen Krieges. Nach Berichten und Urteilen englischer Augenzeugen*, Münster University thesis (1927). E. A. Beller, 'The Military Expedition of Sir Charles Morgan to Germany, 1627–9', *English Historical Review* XLIII (1928). F. L. Carsten, *Princes and Parliaments in Germany* (London, 1959). F. L. Carsten, *The Origins of Prussia* (London, 1954). C. P. Clasen, *The Palatinate in German History* (Oxford, 1964). G. Benecke, *Society and Politics in Germany, 1500–1750* (London, 1974). C. A. Marcartney (ed.), *The Habsburg and Hohenzollern Dynasties* (London, 1970), contains translated documents. B. Chudoba, *Spain and the Empire, 1519–1643* (Chicago, 1952). C. H. Carter, *The Secret Diplomacy of the Habsburgs* (New York, 1965). V. L. Tapié, *The Rise and Fall of the Habsburg Monarchy* (London, 1971), is the best study on this subject. G. E. Rothenburg, *The Austrian Military Border in Croatia, 1522–1747* (Urbana, 1960). R. J. Schleich, *Melchoir Khlesl and the Habsburg Bruderzwist, 1605–12*, Fordham University thesis (1968). H. F. Schwarz, *The Imperial Privy Council in the Seventeenth Century* (Harvard, 1943). M. Reif, *Dignity and Obedience: Social Prestige in the History of the Austrian Habsburgs' Hofkriegsrat* (Kansas, 1964). M. Roberts (ed.), *Sweden's Age of Greatness* (London, 1973). F. H. Schubert, *Ludwig Camerarius* (Kallmünz, 1955), deals with one of the chief advisers to Frederick of the Palatinate. K. Repgen, 'Fabio Chigis Instruktionen für den Westfälischen Friedenskongress', *Römische Quartalschrift* XLVIII (1953), deals with one of the most talented professional diplomats of the period. F. Dickmann, *Der Westfälische Friede* (Münster, 1959), is a classic survey. L. Gross, 'The Peace of Westphalia, 1648–1948', *American Journal of International Law* XLII (1948).

7 Biography

Works on Wallenstein, Gustavus Adolphus and Richelieu dominate, to the unfortunate exclusion of much else. We still await effective biographies on Ferdinand II, Spinola, Infanta Isabella, Tilly and Maximilian of Bavaria – to name only a few.

The enigma of Wallenstein has produced two recent biographies of massive proportions. From the points of view of the historian, probably the less analytical, but certainly the more stylish of the two is now available in English, minus its essential bibliography, and minus an excellent brief appendix on Wallenstein's illnesses pieced together from his apothecary's bills. G. Mann, *Wallenstein* (London, 1976), is a long narrative account. F. Watson, *Wallenstein, Soldier under Saturn* (London, 1938), is another account. For those who read German there is now an analytical biography which avoids none of the source problems: H. Diwald, *Wallenstein. Eine Biographie* (Ullstein paperback, 1975). A. Hollaender, 'Some English Documents on the End of Wallenstein', *Bulletin of the John Rylands Library* XL (1958).

The best biography is of Gustavus Adolphus, namely, M. Roberts, *Gustavus Adolphus* II (London, 1958), which deals with the final months in Germany. See also M. Roberts, 'The Political Objectives of Gustavus Adolphus in Germany, 1630–2', *Transactions of the Royal Historical Society* (1957).

On Richelieu there is a very laborious three-volume study by C. J. Burckhardt, recently translated into English. More useful are L. Weibull, 'Gustave Adolphe et Richelieu', *Revue Historique* CLXXIV (1934), and the important revision of H. Weber, 'Richelieu et le Rhin', *Revue Historique* CCXXXIX (1968). J. H. Elliott, 'The Statecraft of Olivares' in *The Diversity of History* (Festschrift H. Butterfield, Cambridge, 1970). L. Scharffenberg, *Ernst Graf zu Mansfeld* (Gotha, 1867). J. A. Mears, 'Count Raimondo Montecuccoli', *Historian* (1970). T. M. Barker, *The Military Intellectual: Raimondo Montecuccoli and the Thirty Years War* (New York, 1975). C. Oman, *Elizabeth of Bohemia* (London, 1938). O. Mensing (ed.), *Die Bauernchronik des Hartich Sierk aus Wrohm, 1615–64* (Flensburg, 1925). G. Zillhardt (ed.), *Der Dreissigjährige Krieg in Zeitgenössischer Darstellung. Hans Heberles 'Zeytregister' (1618–72). Aufzeichnungen aus dem Ulmer Territorium* (Ulm, 1975), also contains useful notes and tables.

8   *Literature and culture*

H. J. C. von Grimmelshausen, *Simplicius Simplicissimus* (Princeton, 1962, also London, 1964 – different translations), the classic picaresque novel of the Thirty Years War, is best read as light literature in the way in which it was intended; too many academics have tried to take this delightfully scurrilous work too seriously. H. J. C. von Grimmelshausen, *Courage and the False Messiah*, translated by H. Speier (Princeton, 1964), can be usefully read together with Brecht's *Mother Courage*. C. Stoll (ed.), *H. J. C. von Grimmelshausen* (English version, Bonn, 1976). A. Manzoni, *The Betrothed* (Everyman paperback), an early nineteenth-century Italian classic about boy-meets-girl in the turmoil of the Thirty Years War in northern Italy.

Friedrich Schiller's Wallenstein Trilogy is one of the great works of German drama, and it naturally changes historical events, although its interpretations are still among the most perceptive; see *Wallenstein's Death*, edited by M. Esslin, *The Genius of the German Theatre* (Mentor paperback). R. J. Evans, *Rudolf II and his World* (Oxford, 1973). Frances Yates, *The Rosicrucian Enlightenment* (London, 1972). T. Schröder (ed.), *Jacques Callot* (2 vols, Munich, 1971). *The Relation of the Death of the Duke of Friedland*, i.e. Wallenstein (London, 1634, British Library, 1054.b.28). R. J. Evans, 'The Significance of the White Mountain for the Culture of the Czech Lands', *Bulletin of the Institute of Historical Research* 1971.

9 *Religion*

L. Stein, 'Religion and Patriotism in German Peace Dramas during the Thirty Years War', *Central European History* 1971. J. Polišenský: 'Bohemia, the Turk and the Christian Commonwealth', *Byzantinoslavica* XIV. E. Léonard, *History of Protestantism*, translated from the French (London, 1965), contains the best short study on the Thirty Years War. T. Bireley: 'The Peace of Prague (1635) and the Counter-Reformation in Germany', *Journal of Modern History* XLVIII (1976, xerograph for limited circulation). H. C. Midelfort, *Witch Hunting in Southwest Germany* (Stanford, 1972), gives important coverage of the Thirty Years War period. E. Troeltsch, *The Social Teachings of the Christian Churches* (2 vols, London, 1950), is a translation of a classic from the earlier twentieth century. G. Westin, *Negotiations about Church Unity, 1628–34* (Uppsala, 1932). A. Kraus, 'Die auswärtige Politik Urbans VIII', *Festschrift für Kardinal Tisserant* (Vatican, 1964). F. Wolff, *Corpus Catholicorum und Corpus Evangelicorum auf dem Westfälischen Friedenskongress* (Münster, 1966), examines the process whereby (albeit defectively) religion was taken out of German federal-constitutional politics after the 1640s. T. Hoyer, 'The Religious Peace of Augsburg 1555', *Concordia Theological Monthly* XXVI (1955).

10 *Propaganda*

W. A. Coupe, 'Political and Religious Cartoons of the Thirty Years War', *Journal of the Warburg Institute* XXV (1962). W. A. Coupe, *The German Illustrated Broadsheet in the Seventeenth Century* (Baden-Baden, 1966–7); especially important are the illustrations in volume II. E. A. Beller, 'Contemporary English Printed Sources for the Thirty Years War', *American Historical Review* XXXII (1927). E. A. Beller, *Caricatures of the Winter King* (Oxford, 1928). E. A. Beller, *Propaganda in Germany in the Thirty*

Years War (Princeton, 1940). M. Bohatcová (ed.), *Irrgarten der Schicksele.
Einblattdrucke vom Anfang des dreissigjährigen Krieges* (Prague, 1966)..G.
Rystad, *Kriegsnachrichten und Propaganda während des dreissigjährigen Kriegs*
(Lund, 1960), concentrates on Swedish accounts of the Battle of
Nördlingen in 1634. D. Kunzle, *The Early Comic Strip, Narrative Strips and
Picture Stories in the European Broadsheet, 1450–1825*, chapter 3 (Berkeley,
1973).

11   Rebellion

Most of the evidence here is Austrian, and the only brief survey of it in
English is in H. Kamen, *The Iron Century* (London, 1971), a very useful
book for general background. G. Benecke, 'Labour Relations and
Peasant Society in Northwest Germany circa 1600', *History* (October
1973), tries to examine why rebellion did not occur in one locality.
Ausstellungskatalog: Der Oberösterreichische Bauernkrieg, 1626 (Linz, 1976). G.
Pferschy, 'Obersteirische Bauernunruhen, 1635', *Mitteilungen des
steirmärkischen Landesarchivs* XXVI (1976). G. Pferschy, 'Der Streik der
Untertanen (Pogled, 1633)', *Mitteilungen des steirmärkischen Landesarchivs*
XXVI (1971). H. Sturmberger, *Georg Erasmus Tschernembl. Religion, Libertät,
Widerstand* (Graz, 1953), deals with Austrian rebels; there is further
literature in Kamen's *Iron Century*. F. Binder, 'Zum Geschichtsverständnis
der "einfachen Leute"', *Württemberger Jahrbuch für Volkskunde* (1970).

Addenda to the 1984 reprint

To Section 1   *General works*

H. Langer, *The Thirty Years' War* (Poole, 1980), is a translation of an
East German text which combines daring generalizations with excellent illustrations. G. Parker (*et al.*), *The Thirty Years' War* (London,
1984), is the most up-to-date chronologically ordered analysis which
includes full references to further reading. R. J. W. Evans, *The Making
of the Habsburg Monarchy, 1550–1700* (Oxford, 1984), is a definitive
general survey. G. Benecke, in *Histoire sociale-Social History* XIII (Ottawa,
1980), pp. 493–503, reviews new West German interpretations of the
whole early modern period with central focus on the era of the Thirty
Years War. J. W. Zophy (*et al.*), *The Holy Roman Empire: A Dictionary
Handbook* (Westport/Connecticut, 1980), is an efficient work of reference alphabetically arranged with apposite bibliographies. Finally, of
the many new surveys with a wide perspective there is V. G. Kiernan,

State and Society in Europe, 1550–1650 (Oxford, 1980), whilst a very brief structural review comes with G. Benecke, 'The Thirty Years War and its Place in the General Crisis of the Seventeenth Century', *Journal of European Economic History* IX (1980).

To Section 2   *Political thought*

It may be worth taking the more mature reflections on internal political practice as well under this section. M. Raeff, *The Well-ordered Police State: Social and Institutional Change through Law in the Germanies and Russia, 1600–1800* (Yale, 1983), bursts with iconoclasm and unusual comparisons, whilst H. Maier, *Die ältere deutsche Staats- und Verwaltungslehre* (2nd edn, Munich, 1980), remains the standard treatment of German mercantilism, crucial to understanding the legal structure of territorial state politics. Older essays are usefully collected by K. Krüger for O. Hinze, *Beamtentum und Bürokratie* (Göttingen, 1981). Essays 11 to 15 in G. Oestreich, *Neostoicism and the Early Modern State* (Cambridge, 1982), are particularly valuable. Finally, an incisive interpretation of the failure of the 'common man's' political liberty is provided by P. Blickle, *Deutsche Untertanen: ein Widerspruch* (Munich, 1981).

To Section 3   *Economic and social aspects*

Three monographs worth comparing are C. R. Friedrichs, *Urban Society in an Age of War: Nördlingen, 1580–1720* (Princeton, 1979), about the Swabian Imperial city where the Swedes were routed in 1634; G. L. Soliday, *A Community in Conflict: Frankfurt Society in the 17th and Early 18th Centuries* (New Haven, 1974); and M. P. Gutmann, *War and Rural Life in the Early Modern Low Countries* (Princeton, 1980). Classic statements by the Czech historian Hroch on East–West trade and politics are J. Polisensky and M. Hroch, 'Die böhmische Frage und die politischen Beziehungen zwischen dem europäischen Westen und Osten zur Zeit des dreissigjährigen Krieges', in *Problem der Ökonomie und Politik in den Beziehungen zwischen Ost und West Europa* (East Berlin, 1960); M. Hroch, 'Der dreissigjährige Krieg und die europäischen Handelsbeziehungen', *Wissenschaftliche Zeitschrift der Universität Greifswald* XIII (East Germany, 1963). See also J. I. Israel, 'Spanish Wool Exports and the European Economy, 1610–40', *Econ. Hist. Rev.* XXXIII (1981). G. Benecke, 'The Economic Policy of "Kriegsraison" in Germany during the Thirty Years' War', in S. B. and A. H. Vardy, eds., *Society in Change: Studies in Honour of Bela K. Kiraly* (Boulder, 1983).

Finally, there are some clear generalizations in M. Mitterauer and R. Sieder, *The European Family: Patriarchy and Partnership from the Middle Ages to the Present* (Oxford, 1982).

To Section 4   *Collections of documents*

C. A. Macartney, ed., *The Habsburg and Hohenzollern Dynasties* (London, 1970), opens with a number of very useful extracts, as does G. Symcox, ed., *War, Diplomacy and Imperialism, 1618–1763* (London, 1974). On a religious polemical tack, there is a facsimile of the 1614 London edition of *A Declaration of the Faith Professed in the Palatinate* (Amsterdam, 1979).

To Section 5   *Military systems*

Many new studies place the Thirty Years War within a wide perspective, especially the logistical. See M. Duffy, *The Military Revolution and the State, 1500–1800* (University of Exeter Studies in History, 1980); M. van Creveld, *Supplying War* (Cambridge, 1980); A. Corvisier, *Armies and Societies in Europe, 1494–1789* (Bloomington, 1979); M. Howard, *War in European History* (Oxford, 1976). Finally, on the theoretical side: J. T. Johnson, *Just War Tradition and the Restraint of War: A Moral and Historical Inquiry* (Princeton, 1981), contrasts with Heeresgeschichtliches Museum, ed., *Der dreissigjährige Krieg* (Vienna, 1976), on the practical side, studying various specific armies.

To Section 6   *Diplomacy and politics*

A. Attman, *The Struggle for Baltic Markets: Powers in Conflict, 1558–1618* (Gothenburg, 1979), deals with Sweden, Denmark, Poland and Russia. D. Maland, *Europe at War, 1600–50* (London, 1979), provides sound narrative. G. Parker, *Spain and the Netherlands, 1559–1659* (London, 1979), reprints ten very useful articles, worth supplementing with three articles by the late P. J. Brightwell: 'The Spanish System and the Twelve Years' Truce', *EHR* LXXXIX (1974); 'The Spanish Origins of the Thirty Years' War', *Eur. Studs. Rev.* IX (1979); 'Spain, Bohemia and Europe, 1619–21', *Eur. Studs. Rev.* XII (1982). Of major importance is the slim volume by J. H. Elliott, *Richelieu and Olivares* (Cambridge, 1984).

To Section 7   *Biography*

Studies of Gustavus Adolphus are legion, and the anniversary celebration in 1982 produced G. Barudio, *Gustav Adolf der Grosse* (Frankfurt).
The magnificently illustrated catalogue of the Munich exhibition,
'Wittelsbach und Bayern', H. Glaser, ed., *Um Glauben und Reich:
Kurfürst Maximilian I* (2 vols., Munich, 1980), contains the first really
up-to-date treatment of the man in Germany who probably did most to
escalate the Thirty Years War, at least on the Catholic side. See also
A. Kraus, 'Kurfürst Maximilian I von Bayern: das neue Bild eines
grossen Fürsten', *Historisches Jahrbuch* c (1979).

To Section 8   *Literature and culture*

At the Bridge Tavern on the island of Emshagen in Westphalia in 1647
the hostess, Libuschka, wines and dines the German literati of the
1640s, conceived as a parable on the German 1940s by Günter Grass:
The Meeting at Telgte (London, 1983). It is a modern Grimmelshausen
and Brecht could not have done better: a 'must' for those who get tired
of the drier political history of the Thirty Years War. There are some
interesting asides in J. R. Jones, 'English Attitudes to Europe in the
17th Century' in J. S. Bromley and E. H. Kossman, eds., *Britain and the
Netherlands in Europe and Asia* (London, 1968).

To Section 9   *Religion*

The Edict of Restitution, 1629, and much else besides, relives in the
Counter-Reformation high-point with R. Bireley, *Religion and Politics in
the Age of the Counterreformation: Emperor Ferdinand II, William Lamormaini,
S.J., and the Formation of Imperial Policy* (Chapel Hill, 1981). New
interpretations of the 'moderate' German Protestants come with two
articles by B. Nischan: 'Reformed Irenicism and the Leipzig Colloquy
of 1631', *Central European History* ix (1976), and 'Brandenburg's
Reformed *Räte* and the Leipzig Manifesto of 1631', *Journal of Religious
History* x (1979).

To Section 10   *Propaganda*

The first of 10 volumes has appeared of J. R. Paas, *The German Political
Broadsheet, 1600–1700* (Wiesbaden, 1983), covering the years to 1617. It
is a magnificent source as well as a feast for the eyes. Religious and
other early newspaper propaganda is tabulated in Institut für

Zeitungsforschung der Stadt Dortmund, ed., *Pressefrühdrucke aus der Zeit
der Glaubenskämpfe, 1517–1648* (Munich, 1980), whilst there is also an
analysis to go with a chronology of the most significant pamphlets in
K. Vocelka, *Die politische Propaganda Kaiser Rudolfs II, 1576–1612*
(Vienna, 1981).

To Section 11   *Rebellion*

Hermann Rebel, *Peasant Classes: The Bureaucratization of Property and
Family Relations Under Early Habsburg Absolutism* (Princeton, 1983), is
very thought-provoking about the Upper Austrian 1620s and 30s. See
also his article in J. Bak and G. Benecke, eds., *Religion and Rural Revolt*
(Manchester, 1984). Very well-chosen sources of peasants' litigation
and truculence come from W. Schulze, ed., *Bäuerlicher Widerstand und
feudale Herrschaft in der frühen Neuzeit* (Stuttgart, 1980). An East German
psycho-history of sorts is critically promoted by H. Langer, 'Krieges
Alltag und die Bauern: Bemerkungen und Ergänzungen zu Jürgen
Kuczynskis "Geschichte des Alltags des deutschen Volkes" ', *Zeitschrift
für Geschichtsforschung* xxx (1980). Kuczynski's first two volumes
(Cologne, 1980, 1981) are worth persevering with, despite the crude
jumbling and jostling of evidence, often interpreted quite out of
context. Whilst not strictly 'rebellion', we end with the Reformation as
experienced in rural West Germany in an article which, uncommonly,
vividly handles the pastoral archives: T. Robisheaux, 'Peasants and
Pastors: Rural Youth Control and the Reformation in Hohenlohe,
1540–1680', *Social History* vi (1981).